FLOWERS INTO LANDSCAPE

FLOWERS INTO LANDSCAPE

MARGARET STODDART

1865–1934

JULIE KING

ROBERT
McDOUGALL
ART GALLERY
AND ANNEX

HAZARD PRESS
publishers

Guest Curator:	Julie King
Gallery Curatorial Liaison:	Neil Roberts
Editor:	Anna Rogers
Book Design:	Quentin Wilson

Photography:

Lloyd Park
Karl Valpy
Miles Hewton
Auckland Art Gallery
Canterbury Museum
Dunedin Public Art Gallery
Ferner Gallery
Hocken Library, University of Otago, Dunedin
Museum of New Zealand Te Papa Tongarewa
National Library of Australia, Canberra
Nelson Provincial Museum
Photographic Unit, University of Canterbury
Royal Botanic Gardens, Kew
Waikato Museum of Art and History

Lenders:

Public Institutions
Anderson Park Gallery, Invercargill
Auckland Art Gallery
Bishop Suter Art Gallery, Nelson
Canterbury Museum
Christchurch Civic Art Gallery Trust
Christchurch Polytechnic, Te Whare Runanga o Otautahi
Dunedin Public Art Gallery
Forrester Art Gallery, Oamaru
Hocken Library, University of Otago, Dunedin
Manawatu Art Gallery, Palmerston North
Museum of New Zealand Te Papa Tongarewa
Nelson Provincial Museum
Rangi Ruru Girls' School, Christchurch
Robert McDougall Art Gallery
Southland Museum and Art Gallery, Niho o te Taniwha
School of Fine Arts, University of Canterbury
Waikato Museum of Art and History, Te Whare Taonga o Waikato, Hamilton
Private Lenders
Justin Hobbs
Many private collectors who wish to remain anonymous

Photolithography: Digital PrePress Ltd
Printing: Spectrum Print Ltd
ISBN: 1-877161-13-6

Published on the occasion of the exhibition
'*Flowers Into Landscape ~ Margaret Stoddart 1865-1934*'
Robert McDougall Art Gallery, Christchurch
19 November 1997 - 8 February 1998

Frontispiece:
Margaret Stoddart
M. Stoddart Album
Canterbury Museum, Christchurch

CONTENTS

ACKNOWLEDGEMENTS

I wish to record my gratitude to the staff of the Robert McDougall Art Gallery who, under the director, Tony Preston, have supported, co-ordinated and managed this exhibition. Special thanks are due to Quentin Wilson at Hazard Press, and to Anna Rogers for her valuable editorial assistance in the preparation of this publication.

Thanks are also due to the staff of many art galleries, museums and libraries, who have assisted in the realisation of this project, particularly the Canterbury Museum; the New Zealand Room at the Canterbury Public Library; the Macmillan Brown Library, University of Canterbury; the Southland Museum and Art Gallery, Invercargill; the Anderson Park Art Gallery, Invercargill; the Hocken Library, University of Otago; the Dunedin Public Art Gallery; the Forrester Art Gallery, Oamaru; the Aigantighe Art Gallery, Timaru; the Bishop Suter Art Gallery, Nelson; the Nelson Provincial Museum; the Museum of New Zealand Te Papa Tongarewa, Wellington; the Alexander Turnbull Library, National Library of New Zealand, Wellington; the Manawatu Art Gallery, Palmerston North; the Waikato Museum of Art and History, Hamilton; the Auckland Art Gallery; the National Library of Australia, Canberra; the State Library of Victoria, Melbourne; the National Art Library, London; the Library and Archives, Royal Botanic Gardens, Kew; the Edinburgh City Libraries; the Royal Scottish Academy, Edinburgh. I would also like to acknowledge the Friends of Stoddart's Cottage.

Grateful thanks are extended to the individuals who have generously lent works to the exhibition and to the many private owners of paintings whose co-operation has greatly assisted my research.

Thanks are also due to the following individuals for their assistance: Andrew Alston, Roger Blackley, Barbara Brownlie, Julie Catchpole, Fiona Ciaran, Roger Collins, Elizabeth Cumming, Peter Entwisle, Rosemary Entwisle, Kerry Ford, Tim Garrity, Richard Greenaway, Laura van Haven, Vickie Hearnshaw, John Husband, David Kelly, Josie Laing, Tony Lester, Jillian Lloyd, Margaret Lovell-Smith, Kerry McCarthy, Charlotte Macdonald, Judith McKay, Tony Mackle, F.H. MacMillan, Bill Main, Tessa Malcolm, Wayne Marriott, Jenny May, Marian Minson, Eric Pawson, Helene Phillips, Max Podstolski, Jennifer Queree, Maree Ritchie, Michelle Rogan, Michele Slatter, Jo-Anne Smith, Warwick Smith, Joanna Soden, Ashley Sparrow, Marmaduke Spencer Bower, Mary Staplyton-Smith, Lara Strongman, Allan Taylor, Helen Telford, Joe Torr, Jill Trevelyan, Tina Troup, Linda Tyler, Marion Whybrow, Pam Wilson, John Wilson, Joan Woodward. Finally, I would like to acknowledge my colleagues and students at the School of Fine Arts.

JULIE KING

Director's Foreword

'…I forgot the weather amongst Miss Stoddart's beautiful flower paintings in the Art Gallery. I had the pleasure of meeting her, and next morning went to see her whole collection. It was a new revelation to me to see such work hidden away, and I think she stands without rival the first and foremost of our flower painters… Her grouping, colouring, form and harmony were perfect.' (Ellis Rowan, *A Flower-Hunter in Queensland and New Zealand,* Sydney, 1898, p.251)

This was rare and gracious praise from a fellow flower painter, who was far better known for her competitive nature, her barely disguised ambition and her determined development and use of influential friends. The Canterbury-born artist who inspired these comments was Margaret Olrog Stoddart and in 1940, six years after her death, E.H. McCormick noted that 'Miss Stoddart's roses' had become 'part of the tradition of New Zealand painting…'

Of all Stoddart's work it was the still-life painting of various flora that established her, but any notion of her as merely another genteel flower painter is refuted by the range and breadth of her oeuvre, and by her determined pursuit of a successful artistic career. She belonged to the first generation of New Zealand women who succeeded in establishing themselves as professional artists, and she stands out sharply among her contemporaries for the individual direction she took in landscape painting.

This is the first major exhibition of Margaret Stoddart's work since 1935 and it is appropriate that it has been organised by the Robert McDougall Art Gallery.

An exhibition of this calibre and scale is possible only with the research, support and advice of many people, and I acknowledge and commend to you the work of Julie King, guest curator and author, and Neil Roberts, whose special efforts as co-curator in tracking down key works in private hands, required sleuth-like tenacity on several occasions.

I thank the many lenders, both public and private, without whose willingness to share their treasures these exhibitions cannot happen, and Creative New Zealand and Harcourts, whose belief in the significance of this tour saw the former generously support this catalogue, and the latter, the exhibition poster and other related publications.

Finally, I wish to record my appreciation of the efforts of many of the McDougall staff who have turned a curatorial concept into rewarding reality. My thanks, and my congratulations to you all.

P. Anthony Preston
Director, Robert McDougall Art Gallery

CHRONOLOGY AND EXHIBITIONS

Abbreviations ASA – Auckland Society of Arts, CSA – Canterbury Society of Arts, NZAFA – New Zealand Academy of Fine Arts, OAS – Otago Art Society.

1865

Margaret Olrog Stoddart is born at Diamond Harbour on 3 October, and is baptised 1 November at Holy Trinity, Lyttelton, Canterbury. She is the second daughter of Anna Barbara Schjött and her husband, Mark Pringle Stoddart. Their son, Mark Sprot, died aged two years old, on 26 May. Their eldest daughter, Frances, was born in the previous year on 26 July 1864.

1866

On 17 April, Margaret and her older sister, Frances, leave with their parents from Lyttelton on the *Himalaya* to visit relatives in Scotland. They arrive in Edinburgh on 31 July.

1867

In June and July, Mark and Anna Stoddart take their children on a visit to Anna's family in Norway. The couple leave England on the *Glenmark* with Frances, Margaret and newly born James. They arrive at Lyttelton on 14 November, and return to Diamond Harbour.

1868

Mary is born 27 June and baptised 1 August at Holy Trinity, Lyttelton. Margaret Schjött is the child's sponsor.

1869

Agnes is born 10 December and baptised at Holy Trinity, Lyttelton on 20 January 1870. Ernestine Schjött is the child's sponsor.

1872

John Schjött Stoddart is born on 3 April and baptised on 23 April at Holy Trinity, Lyttelton.

1876

On 15 April, the Stoddarts leave Diamond Harbour and sail from Lyttelton on the *Jessie Osborne*. They arrive in Edinburgh in July, and Margaret and Frances enrol at the Merchant Maiden School in Queen Street, Edinburgh.

1879

The Stoddarts leave England on 21 June, travelling as saloon passengers on the *Crusader,* commanded by Captain Llewellyn Davies, and arrive at Lyttelton on 24 September.

1880

The Stoddart family take up residence at Lismore Lodge, Fendalton, Christchurch.

1882

Margaret enrols with her sisters Frances, Mary and Agnes in the Morning Class at the Canterbury College School of Art, where she studies under David Blair and George Herbert Elliott. Fellow students include Kate Sheppard, Marie Beath, Samuel H. Seager, the architect, and Rosa Budden (later Sawtell). At the end of the year she gains passes in freehand drawing and model drawing.

1883

Margaret and her sisters continue their studies at the Canterbury College School of Art. On 30 January, Margaret becomes a working member of the CSA.
Exhibitions: CSA.

1884

Margaret's attendance at the school is interrupted and she registers for the second term only.
Exhibitions: ASA, CSA, OAS.

1885

In March, the CSA purchases 127, *Mountain Lily* and 130, *Roses* from the CSA Annual Exhibition. On 28 August, Mark Stoddart dies at home, aged 66. He is buried at St Peter's, Riccarton on 1 September. Later that month Margaret becomes a member of the council of the CSA, a position which she holds until 1889. Frances is awarded the Second Grade Full Certificate from the Canterbury College School of Art.
Exhibitions: ASA, CSA, OAS.

1886

On 19 April, Margaret arrives at the Chatham Islands where she stays with Edward and Mabel Chudleigh at Wharekauri. She gains the Auckland Society of Arts Silver Medal for a watercolour study in flowers and foliage.
Exhibitions: ASA, CSA, OAS.
London, Colonial and Indian Exhibition (4 works: *Paintings of New Zealand Flowers: Mountain Daisies; In the Bush: Yellow Kowai; Native Clematis; Native Coltsfoot*).

1887

On 24 January, she travels to Pitt Island and, from 28 February until 26 March, she stays with the Shands at Te Whakaru. She leaves Waitangi on 7 June on the *Kahu*, and arrives at Lyttelton on 9 June. She resumes her studies at the Canterbury College School of Art in the third term. Her teachers include George Herbert Elliott and Alfred Wilson Walsh. In November, the Canterbury Museum purchases two pictures of Chatham Island scenery.
Exhibitions: CSA, OAS.

1888

Margaret continues her studies at the School of Art and works in the life class. Dora Meeson is a fellow student. She designs two

Christmas cards, *New Zealand Sunrise* and *View on West Coast,* for A.D. Willis, Chromo-Lithographer and Bookseller, Wanganui. She is awarded the Otago Art Society prize for 195, *Study from Life. A Beach Comber*, and the Auckland Society of Arts Bronze Medal.
Exhibitions: ASA, CSA, OAS.

1889

In January, she visits her friend Nina Jones, a flower painter in Nelson. She registers at the School of Art as a free student, and at the end of the year she is awarded the Second Grade Full Certificate and a Free Studentship. She gains first prize for a study of a head from life at the Auckland Society of Arts. Fellow students include Dora Meeson and Edith E. Munnings. Frances registers in May at the Canterbury College for the degree of BA.
Exhibitions: CSA, ASA, NZAFA.
Dunedin, New Zealand and South Seas Exhibition (3 works: 116, *Folding Screen (upon each panel are representations of New Zealand flora)*; 18, *Owenja Cliffs*; 46, *Apricot Blossom).*

1890

She attends the School of Art as a free student, and leaves at the end of the year. Dora Meeson leaves mid-year. In March, the Canterbury Museum purchases 12 drawings of New Zealand flowers from Margaret for £6.
Exhibitions: CSA, ASA, NZAFA.

1891

In April, Margaret travels in a party accompanying Bishop Churchill Julius to the Chatham Islands, where she attends the consecration of St Augustine's at Te One on 5 April. She stays on with the Chud-leighs at Wharekauri until 10 July, and arrives at Lyttelton on 12 July.
Exhibitions: CSA, ASA, NZAFA.

1892

In August, Margaret joins a party to climb Mount Torlesse, which takes them 7 hours. The excursion, organised by Mr and Mrs Olliver, includes Mr and Mrs Westland, Miss Lean, Miss Harper, Messrs Harman, Graham, Black and Mannering.
Exhibitions: CSA, ASA, OAS, NZAFA.

1893

In January, Margaret travels to Wellington, and visits the Rangiatea Church at Otaki. She climbs Mount Torlesse in August. In November, Marmaduke Dixon, G.E. Mannering and Tom Fyfe attempt to climb Mount Cook.
Exhibitions: CSA, OAS, NZAFA.

1894

Margaret is a member of the council of the CSA, a position which she holds until 1897. She gives drawing and painting classes at her studio, Hobbs' Buildings, Christchurch. In March or April she meets Ellis Rowan in Christchurch. She travels to Melbourne in August, where she holds an exhibition in October. She returns home around November via Tasmania.
Exhibitions: CSA.
Melbourne, James Peele's studio, Old City Court, Swanston Street (30 works).

1895

Dora Meeson leaves to study at the National Gallery School at Melbourne.
Exhibitions: CSA, NZAFA, OAS.

1896

In April, she travels with Rosa Dixon and others on an expedition along the West Coast Road.
Exhibitions: ASA, CSA, NZAFA, OAS.

1897

Margaret moves with her mother and sisters from Lismore Lodge, Fendalton, and returns to live at Diamond Harbour. Her sister, Frances, takes up the position of headmistress at Toi Toi Valley School, Nelson.
Exhibitions: CSA, NZAFA, OAS.

1898

Margaret arrives in England, and makes contact with Dora Meeson, who is living in London. This year, or possibly in 1899, she travels to Norway.
Exhibitions: CSA.
Birmingham, Royal Birmingham Society of Artists (1 work: 556, *Wall Flowers* £12 12s).

1899

She exhibits in March as a pupil of Louis Grier at his studio at St Ives in Cornwall. While she is in Europe she also takes lessons with Norman Garstin and Charles Lasar, and makes several sketching trips on the continent. Later this year, or in 1900, she visits France and Switzerland.
Exhibitions: London, Royal Institute of Painters in Water Colours (1 work: 129, *Sweet Violets* £5 5s).
London, Royal Society of British Artists (2 works: 338, *Wallflowers, New Zealand* £8 8s; 468, *A Cottage Door* £5 5s).
Birmingham, Royal Birmingham Society of Artists (3 works: 56, *Land and Sea* £15 15s; 458, *Cornish Mine Country* £10 10s; 756, *Sweet Violets* £5 5s).

1900

Exhibitions: CSA, OAS.
Christchurch, Canterbury Jubilee Industrial Exhibition (3 works: 82, *Scene of Shakespeare*; 208, *Shirley Poppies*; 243, *Primroses and Violets).*

London, Royal Society of British Artists (2 works: 366, *On the Edge of the Moor* £10 10s; 490, *Chrysanthemums* £5 5s).

1901

James Stoddart dies on 17 January at Bulawayo, South Africa. Frances Hodgkins and Rosa Dixon arrive in England in April, and Rosa registers at the Slade School of Drawing, Painting and Sculpture. Margaret arranges to meet Frances in London on 3 June. In November, she is at St Ives.

Exhibitions: ASA, CSA, NZAFA.

1902

Margaret is visited in March at St Ives by Frances Hodgkins and Dorothy Richmond. She exhibits her paintings on Show Day at St Ives. Later that year she visits France, and paints *Camiero, France,* dated 1902 (Robert McDougall Art Gallery). Margaret's sister, Frances, resigns from her teaching post with the intention of travelling to Europe early next year.

Exhibitions: CSA, OAS.

London, Baillie Gallery. Fellow exhibitors include Frances Hodgkins, Grace Joel, Dorothy Richmond.

Paris, Société des Artistes Français (1 work: 2154, *Les narcisses*).

1903

In April, Margaret exhibits on Show Day at St Ives. In June, she works at Bushey, Hertfordshire, where she meets Frances Hodgkins.

Exhibitions: CSA, OAS.

Paris, Société des Artistes Français (1 work: 2424, *Les pavots.*)

1904

In March, she exhibits on Show Day at St Ives.

Exhibitions: CSA, NZAFA.

Paris, Société des Artistes Français (2 works: 2549, *Les roses d'été*; 2550, *Les rosettes*).

1905

Margaret works in the summer at Suffolk and Norfolk. During the year she spends time in Italy, and paints at Venice, Siena, Rome and Capri. Frances takes up a position as teacher at Motueka District High School, where she remains until 1915.

The CSA purchases 211, *Camiero, France* from the CSA Annual Exhibition.

Exhibitions: ASA, CSA, NZAFA.

Paris, Société Nationale des Beaux-Arts (1 work: 1648, *Les narcisses*).

1906

In March, Margaret exhibits on Show Day at St Ives. She spends the summer months in Suffolk and Norfolk, before leaving for New Zealand in November.

Exhibitions: CSA, NZAFA.

London, Royal Academy (1 work: 1045, *A Capri Garden*).

London, The Society of Women Artists (2 works: 90, *Daffodils and Narcissus* £8 8s; 109, *Bluebells* £6 6s).

London, Baillie Gallery (39 works)

Paris, Société Nationale des Beaux-Arts (1 work: 1678, *Les roses de Noël.*)

Christchurch, New Zealand International Exhibition (5 works: 236, *Roses* £5 5s; 253, *A Capri Street* £5 5s; 262, *A Capri Villa* £5 5s; 265, *Canal, Venice* £5 5s; 274, *Old Cottages, Beccles* £5 5s; 276, *Storm Clouds, Blythburgh Suffolk* £5 5s).

1907

Margaret passes through Wellington in January, and returns to Diamond Harbour where she lives with her mother and sisters. On 18 March, she presents a collection of drawings of plants to the Canterbury Museum.

Exhibitions: ASA, CSA, OAS.

1908

Mary Stoddart marries Richard Farques Farmer on 4 September at Holy Trinity, Lyttelton. Her brother, John, who is living in Rhodesia, attends the wedding.

Exhibitions: ASA, CSA, NZAFA.

1909

Margaret sketches with Cora Wilding. On 16 October, Mary gives birth to a daughter, Frances Stoddart Mary Farques Farmer, but dies after childbirth and is buried on 22 October at Holy Trinity, Lyttelton.

Exhibitions: CSA, NZAFA.

Paris, Société des Artistes Français (2 works: 2851, *Les roses*; 2852, *Les roses*).

1910

Exhibitions: CSA, NZAFA, OAS.

Paris, Société des Artistes Français (2 works: 3110, *La pluie sur les côtes*; 3111, *Les eucalyptus*).

1911

Anna Barbara Stoddart dies aged 76 on 6 June and is buried on 8 June at St Peter's, Riccarton.

Exhibitions: CSA, OAS, NZAFA.

Christchurch, CSA Gallery, October, one-person exhibition (50 works).

1912

The CSA purchases 289, *Anna Ollivier Roses* from the CSA Annual Exhibition.

Exhibitions: CSA, OAS.

Paris, Société des Artistes Français (1 work: 3066, *Sur les côtes (Bank's Peninsule)*).

1913

In 1913-14, the Lyttelton Borough Council purchases 336 acres of land at Diamond Harbour from the trustees, Margaret and Frances. Margaret's address is given as 6 Dublin Street, Christchurch in the Annual Exhibition Catalogue of the CSA.

Exhibitions: ASA, CSA, OAS, NZAFA.

Paris, Société des Artistes Français (2 works: 2971, *Après l'orage*; 2972, *Le courant*).

1914

Margaret moves with Agnes to Hackthorne Road, Christchurch.

Exhibitions: CSA, NZAFA.

Paris, Société des Artistes Français (1 work: 3272, *Les dunes*).

1915

Exhibitions: ASA, CSA, OAS, NZAFA.

1916

Exhibitions: CSA, OAS, NZAFA.

1917

Exhibitions: CSA, OAS, NZAFA.

1918

Exhibitions: CSA, OAS, NZAFA.

1919

Exhibitions: CSA, NZAFA.

1920

Margaret spends Easter sketching at Mount Ruapehu with Dorothy Richmond. During the 1920s, she also sketches with Rosa and Olivia Spencer Bower, and is a member of the Canterbury Women's Club, the Society for Imperial Culture and the Sketch Club.

Exhibitions: ASA, CSA, NZAFA, OAS.

1921

Exhibitions: CSA, NZAFA, OAS.

1922

Exhibitions: ASA, CSA, NZAFA, OAS.

1923

Exhibitions: CSA, NZAFA, OAS.

Paris, Société des Artistes Français (1 work: 2618, *The Silent Pool*).

1924

The CSA purchases 106, *Low Tide Akaroa* from the CSA Annual Exhibition. The NZAFA purchases 205, *Roses* from the NZAFA Annual Exhibition. At the end of this year, or in 1925, she travels to Tahiti and Sydney, Australia.

Exhibitions: ASA, CSA, NZAFA.

London, British Empire Exhibition, Wembley (1 work: 15, *A New Zealand Stream* £15 15s).

1925

Margaret Stoddart becomes a member of the National Art Association of New Zealand.

Exhibitions: ASA, CSA, OAS.

London, British Empire Exhibition (3 works: *In the Otira Valley*; *The Rose Garden, Christchurch*; *A Peninsula Gully*).

Paris, Société des Artistes Français (1 work: 1506, *The Waterfront, Papeete*).

Dunedin, International Exhibition of Fine Arts, New Zealand and South Seas International Exhibition (1 work: 8, *Smiling Morn*).

1926

John Stoddart dies in Rhodesia.

Exhibitions: ASA, CSA, NZAFA, OAS.

Paris, Société des Artistes Français (2 works: 2970, *Melting Snows 'Neige fondante'*; 2971, *The Argyll Cut*).

Sydney, Australian Water Colour Institute Annual Exhibition at the Education Department Galleries, Loftus Street (3 works: 33, *The Argyle Cut* £10 10s; 56, *La Fête, Tahiti* £10 10s; 57, *Beach* £10 10s). Fellow exhibitors include Thea Proctor, Maud Sherwood and Vida Lahey.

1927

Exhibitions: ASA, CSA, NZAFA, OAS.

Paris, Société des Artistes Français (2 works: 2835, *The Franz Joseph* [sic] *Glacier*; 2836, *Old Warf, Akarva* [sic]).

1928

Exhibitions: CSA, NZAFA, OAS.

Christchurch, Canterbury Society of Arts Gallery, An Exhibition of Past and Present Work by Miss M.O. Stoddart (198 works).

Paris, Société des Artistes Français (2 works: 2944, *Le lit de la Rivière Waiho*; 2945, *Vent d'Est*).

1929

Margaret is elected to the council of the CSA.

Exhibitions: CSA, NZAFA, OAS.

1930

The NZAFA purchases 126, *Roses* from the NZAFA Annual Exhibition.

Exhibitions: CSA, NZAFA.

Paris, Société des Artistes Français (2 works: 3028, *Neige*; 3029, *Montagne fleurie*).

1931

Margaret serves as vice-president of the CSA, a position she holds until her death.

Exhibitions: CSA, NZAFA.

1932

Exhibitions: ASA, CSA, NZAFA, OAS.

1933

She is at Otira, where she spends time with Cora Wilding.

Exhibitions: CSA, NZAFA, OAS.

1934

Margaret dies from a heart attack on 10 December at Hanmer. Her funeral is held at St Augustine's Church, Cashmere, and she is buried on 12 December at Bromley Cemetery, Christchurch.

Exhibitions: CSA, NZAFA.

1935

Exhibitions: Christchurch, Canterbury Society of Arts Gallery, Exhibition of Paintings by the late Miss M.O. Stoddart (206 works) in June.

Wellington, NZAFA Gallery, Exhibition of Paintings by the late Miss M.O.Stoddart (117 works) in July.

Auckland, The Art Gallery, Loan Collection of Water-Colour Paintings by the Late Miss M.O. Stoddart (110 works) in November.

INTRODUCTION

For five decades Margaret Stoddart was arguably this country's best-known flower painter. Beginning in the 1880s with precisely observed studies of native plants pictured frequently in their natural habitats, she moved on to delicately painted still lifes and, by the early 1900s, her painterly techniques meant that she was well on the way to making this genre her own. In her maturity, the play of reflections and colour harmonies, so distinctive in her still lifes, found full expression in resplendent arrangements of roses, their transience caught in the fragility of full bloom. In 1940, six years after her death, E.H. McCormick observed in his centennial survey, *Letters and Art in New Zealand*, that, along with the still lifes of zinnias by Dorothy Richmond, '…Miss Stoddart's roses have become part of the tradition of New Zealand painting, as representative of the taste and achievement of their time as Gully's landscapes are of his'.[1]

Margaret Stoddart's flower paintings appear to be simpler than they are and it is their very accessibility which has discouraged serious consideration of their significance or of that of the artist herself.[2] Her beginnings as a flower painter were shaped by women's artistic culture and by colonial society's widespread interest in the indigenous plants of New Zealand. A curiosity about native flora gave female artists the incentive to practise in this area and Margaret made numerous expeditions into the back country to paint alpine plants. In 1886 and again in 1891, she travelled to the Chatham Islands and, after meeting the successful Australian flower painter, Ellis Rowan, in

Bowl of Roses
Watercolour and bodycolour
460 × 590mm
Collection of Dunedin Public Art Gallery

14

Garden, Christchurch, (c.1912)
Watercolour and bodycolour over charcoal
254 × 354mm
Collection of Hocken Library, University of Otago, Dunedin

Christchurch, she made a trip to Melbourne where she held her own exhibition in 1894. Several years later she left to work in Europe and to establish herself as a professional artist.

Although Margaret's reputation was gained initially as a flower painter, before leaving New Zealand she had developed a keen interest in landscape and in working outdoors. But it was during her time in Europe, from 1898 until 1906, that landscape themes first began to feature prominently. While she was based in Cornwall at the artists' colony of St Ives, which was home to a school of landscapists, her interests broadened to include many of the characteristic motifs favoured in British Impressionism, such as harbour scenes, orchards in blossom and a range of rural and seasonal themes. Leaving Europe in 1906, she returned to New Zealand for what was intended to be only a temporary stay, but ended up settling here for the rest of her life. She then turned to her own environment.

By the turn of the century, paintings of spectacular scenery had given way to the depiction of familiar places and this opened up greater opportunities for female painters to practise as landscapists. Margaret painted

House in a Summer Garden
Watercolour and bodycolour over charcoal
242 × 342mm
Collection of Forrester Gallery, Oamaru,
gifted by the North Otago Art Society

impressionist scenes close to home, around the bay at Diamond Harbour in the Lyttelton inlet, at the seaside resorts of New Brighton and Sumner and in the city's parks and gardens. These images recorded the urban and suburban landscapes established during the artist's lifetime and expressed her developing experience of European settlement. She also worked further afield and, from the 1920s, presented her public with two distinct environments: a benign landscape of gardens, parks and suburban countryside, where nature is cultivated and easily accessible; and the hinterland, with its mountain gullies and stony riverbeds, images that affirmed her audience's growing awareness of a local identity.

Margaret's career spanned fifty years and covered a broad range of floral and landscape subjects, yet the way in which ideas about the different nature of men's and women's art pertained to her work is seen in a generous tribute written after her death by James Shelley and Sydney Thompson:

> Miss Stoddart was one of Nature's artists…with a strong, healthy outlook that amounted almost to masculinity…she was especially successful with scenes that were rather stark and untamed, like the swirling waters of the shingly river-beds

of Canterbury. Her flower pieces were always greatly appreciated, but one felt there was a sterner reality about the painting than the fragile flowers themselves possessed. There was nothing fragile about Miss Stoddart, but rather a sort of tender violence. Even the medium she worked in – watercolour – seemed to lack the strength she sought, and she was frequently led to trespass into the realms of bodycolour in search for a more dynamic utterance. [3]

This book seeks to illuminate Margaret Stoddart's painting in relation to its time, and to add to our understanding of how women worked as artists. Like Frances Hodgkins, Margaret belonged to an expatriate generation, but, unlike her more famous contemporary, she came home. Her considerable popularity during her lifetime and with later private collectors has contrasted with her neglect by historians. E.H. McCormick correctly observed that Margaret Stoddart was one of a number of 'very interesting women artists' of whom only limited records had remained.[4] As with many women painters of this period, few of her personal papers have survived, deliberately or accidentally, but some insight into her early life can be found in a fragmentary correspondence with a friend and fellow artist, Rosa Dixon, and in the albums of Margaret and her sister, Mary.

By drawing on these records and from a range of other sources, this book traces Margaret's background and social origins, the arrival of her family in New Zealand in the mid-nineteenth century, her training as a foundation student at the Canterbury College School of Art, how she exhibited and sold

An Otira Stream, also known as *Mountain Rata,* (c. 1927)
Watercolour and bodycolour over charcoal
430 x 460mm
Collection of Robert McDougall Art Gallery, Christchurch

View of Mount Cook
Watercolour and bodycolour over charcoal
450 × 480mm
Auckland Art Gallery Collection

her work, her visit to Melbourne and experiences working in Europe and her practice as a flower painter and landscapist.

This publication coincides with the exhibition, *Flowers into Landscape: Margaret Stoddart 1865-1934,* organised by the Robert McDougall Art Gallery, which is the first major showing of the artist's work to have taken place since 1935. Stoddart's practice as a flower painter had a special bearing on her perception, and this is revealed in landscape painting in her sense of the vividness and variety of nature in a rapidly changing environment. A consideration of her work in relation to shifting artistic and cultural contexts reveals how her landscape and flower paintings were 'representative of the taste and achievement of their time'.

NOTES:

1. E.H. McCormick, *Letters and Art in New Zealand*, Wellington, 1940, p.159.

2. Ann Elias pioneered the consideration of flower painting in New Zealand in her thesis: Ann Elias, 'New Zealand Still Life and Flower Painting 1880-1940', unpublished PhD thesis, University of Auckland, 1991.

3. Sydney L. Thompson and J. Shelley, 'Miss M.O. Stoddart', *Art in New Zealand*, Vol. VIII, No. 2, December 1935, pp.99, 100-101.

4. Michael King, 'Not Quite One of the Boys', in *Writing a New Country*, edited by James Ross, Linda Gill and Stuart McRae, Auckland, 1933, p.27.

The Emergence of a Colonial Woman Artist

Margaret Olrog Stoddart belonged to the first generation of colonial artists born in New Zealand, and she became one of the first women to succeed as a professional painter in this country.[1] Her appearance among a cluster of talented and promising female artists, who included Dorothy Richmond (1861-1935), Grace Joel (1865-1924) and Frances Hodgkins (1869-1947), makes an interesting episode in the history of colonial art, although the emergence of women painters around this time was by no means a uniquely New Zealand phenomenon. Economic pressures and social changes in the late nineteenth century provided middle-class women with greater opportunities to pursue artistic careers and a remarkable number of parallels can be drawn between the experiences of female painters here and their counterparts in Australia, Canada and the American West.[2] In that period of transition, when new ideas about the role of women and traditional expectations co-existed, professional ambitions came into conflict with ideals of femininity and women artists often faced disapproval and found themselves occupying an ambiguous position within art institutions. In this context, exploring the careers of individual painters adds to our understanding of what it meant to assume the identity of a professional artist.

Margaret Stoddart's emergence as an artist was gradual and discreet and it began in her childhood. She came from an enterprising and cultivated family that placed a high value on art and education, and her upbringing was of the utmost importance in stimulating her artistic aspirations. Her father was a landowner and, through his interest in natural history and his connections with Thomas Henry Potts and Julius von Haast, two scientists whose wide-ranging research and detailed observations contributed to nineteenth-century knowledge about the colony, she was introduced in her youth to a view of the natural world that shaped and enlarged her understanding of her surroundings. Growing up during the 1860s and 1870s at Diamond Harbour, Canterbury, in a rapidly changing physical environment, had an important bearing on Margaret's experience of landscape and on her painting.

The Stoddarts in New Zealand

Margaret was born at Diamond Harbour, Canterbury, on 3 October 1865, to Anna Barbara Schjött and her husband, Mark Pringle Stoddart. Her mother, the daughter of a clergyman from Skien in southern Norway, came from a large family with limited means, and she had emigrated to New Zealand as a governess when she was twenty-five years old. She was listed as one of thirty-four unmarried female passengers who sailed to Canterbury

Reverend Henry Torlesse.
Canterbury Museum, Christchurch

Elizabeth Torlesse.
Canterbury Museum, Christchurch

on the SS *Matoaka* in 1860 on an assisted emigration scheme.[3] During the 1850s and 1860s, around 12,000 single women travelled to this country as assisted immigrants; 8000 of them came to Otago and to the Canterbury Province, which was considered an orderly and very respectable colonial destination.[4] E.C. Richards's brief notes in E.R. Chudleigh's diary outlined a familiar story of personal contacts, respectability and the reduced circumstances that may have precipitated Anna's removal to New Zealand: 'Anna Schjott [*sic*] pa preacher no money large family… Heard of N.Z. through Wards Crosbie… Anna taught Ward girls in Ireland. Came to N.Z. with Miss Weale and perhaps Miss F Torlesse…'[5]

The SS *Matoaka* made a rapid and pleasant passage of eighty-eight days and landed at Lyttelton on 2 December 1860,[6] and shortly afterwards, Anna and Doratea Weale, a first-class passenger on the ship, paid a visit to Okains Bay to meet the Reverend Henry Torlesse. Charlotte Julia Doratea Weale was a philanthropist and benefactor with connections in the Anglican church and her visit to New Zealand was probably related to her involvement in the welfare of immigrant women.[7] Henry Torlesse, a nephew of Edward Gibbon Wakefield and a brother of Charles Torlesse, a surveyor for the Canterbury Association, had been ordained in 1859 as deacon of the parish at Okains Bay and its neighbouring settlements, and he had gone there with his wife, Elizabeth, to establish the church and provide schooling for the growing population. It was the largest settlement among the bays along the eastern coast of Banks Peninsula, and during the 1850s men had drifted into the area, attracted by the chance of employment in bush felling. When the Torlesses arrived, the bay's inhabitants numbered about 144 and included, according to Henry's reports, an unruly and disorderly element.[8] Anna joined them as a teacher at the chapel school and found her place as a single woman in a new society working for the educational improvement and good of the community.

While Anna was at Okains Bay, she and Elizabeth Torlesse became close companions.[9] Many years later, Elizabeth described her friend's arrival, setting the event tellingly within the harsh realities and vicissitudes of an earlier pioneering time:

> In 1861 our second daughter Susan Bridget was born and before I was about a Miss Neale [*sic*] and Miss Schott [*sic*] came from Christchurch to pay us a visit and see what a rough life in the Bay was like. They stayed for a month and then returned to Lyttelton on Easter Monday. The men that came for them on a whaleboat were upset on the bar and drowned. Henry had been ill with a bad sore throat but was better and he and the two ladies left in a timber boat, Easter Monday morning taking the bodies of the two men with them to Lyttelton. Henry could not take any services that week as he could only speak in a whisper. It was a sad time. Miss Schott [*sic*] decided to return to help with the school work – she had kindly taken it on for a fortnight while Henry was ill. She lived with us for a year and was married at the Bay to Mr Stoddart of Diamond Harbour Lyttelton.[10]

Anna Schjött and Mark Stoddart were married by the Reverend Torlesse at the chapel school on 27 February 1862. Mark Stoddart's friend and neighbour at Governors Bay, Thomas Potts, acted as best man and the wedding was remembered as an important social occasion:

> [Mr Stoddart] brought his friends down to the Bay in a steamer and it was a glorious day. We had a large tent put up and we entertained all the married people in the Bay and after that the children. The bride was such a favourite with everyone. They left with their friends in the afternoon by steamer and we kept the wedding festivities going on till 9 p.m. It was a great day for the Bay. Mrs Stoddart took a great interest in the work going on in the Bay and she came to see us on two occasions, walking over the hills. We missed her very much.[11]

The marriage was a practical and advantageous partnership within the restricted circles of 1860s colonial society. Anna's education and religious upbringing earned respect, and the hardships and trials of her emigrant experience proved a testing preparation for her future life. At the time of his marriage Mark Stoddart was forty-three, sixteen years older than his wife, but his age was offset by his social position, which was defined variously in registers as farmer, stockholder, JP and gentleman. The youngest son of an admiral in Edinburgh and a gentleman by birth, he had emigrated in 1837 at the age of eighteen to Port Phillip in Australia, where he had set himself up as a pastoralist in Victoria. Stoddart was one of a number of runholders who sold up their stations during the prolonged droughts of the early 1850s and, attracted by the potential for pastoralism in Canterbury, crossed the Tasman to try their luck in the new settlement. Joining up with his friend, E.M. Templar, and sailing with a stock of 2000 sheep, he arrived at Lyttelton in January 1851.[12] Exploring inland, he travelled up the Rakaia where he established a sheep-run, taking out a lease in August for 20,000 acres for Run 20, Rakaia Terrace.[13]

Mark Pringle Stoddart.
Canterbury Museum, Christchurch

Early in the following year Mark Stoddart was visited by the Canterbury Association's chief agent, John Robert Godley. He later recalled his initial reception by Godley and the '…sort of eyeing askance with which he was first regarded as an interloping squatter'.[14] Godley's attitude to their meeting hints at differences in outlook between the association's recent emigrants, known as Canterbury Pilgrims, and the 'shagroons', those experienced Australian squatters, like Mark Stoddart, whom Godley treated initially with some distrust. Stoddart's rough accommodation and manner of living appear to have confirmed Godley's apprehension about the lowering tendencies of colonial life.

Charlotte Godley's account of her husband's visit to Stoddart's run reveals some of the difficulties that he evidently experienced in dealing with a man whose outlook had been shaped by fifteen years of familiarity with pioneering conditions:

My husband got safely back from his journey up the country, yesterday… The last night he was out at Deans' station, where there was no sort of candle, which does not do when you have thirteen hours of darkness, as we have now. The morning before was most uncomfortable; they were at the station of a Mr. Stoddart, who came here from Port Phillip, and although he has been here about a year, he still lives in a horrible den, or cabin, into which you creep through a hole; there being neither door nor window. The floor was of liquid mud, and on the best bit of it they spent the night… Imagine yourself getting up after such a night, and finding yourself obliged to go down to the river to wash, through two inches deep of snow (in which form the storm we had here fell among the mountains); thereby completely and irretrievably wetting your feet. The alternative was to get up and shake yourself, and content yourself with washing on fine mornings, about twice a week. I believe it is rather the Australian plan to live in this discomfort, unless there is a lady concerned; but it seems the more extraordinary because Mr. Stoddart appears to have money, and it would certainly cost very few shillings to make a wonderful change as to cleanliness. I can hardly believe still there was no window! There was one, let us hope, but without glass; only a shutter which was shut for bad weather!! And he is, moreover, when he appears in the world, quite a gentlemanlike man, fond of drawing, poetry, reading and so on; and so clever and pleasant, that he made them spend a very agreeable evening, in spite of the locality.[15]

Stoddart's background granted him entry into early Canterbury society, and he was acquainted with many of its leading figures, including Godley's associate, future premier Henry Sewell, an astute observer of his contemporaries, who described him as '…a Port Phillip Squatter lately settled in Canterbury on a sheep station – a man of good family – held in considerable estimation, and according to Wakefield's account likely to be a leader here'.[16]

Stoddart's cottage, Diamond Harbour, 1890s.
M. Stoddart Album, Canterbury Museum, Christchurch

But despite Stoddart's prior experience as a runholder and a propitious arrival in Canterbury, his sheep-farming ventures were not successful by the standards of their time. Discouraged by an inclement climate, he declared himself 'tired of station life', and after two seasons transferred the pasturage licence at Rakaia Terrace, with 1870 sheep and lambs, horses, improvements and stores, to John Hall for £2,750.[17] In his next undertaking, he was caught by the uncertainties of land-pricing systems outside the association's Canterbury Block and, after joining Robert Waitt in a partnership at Glenmark, which was co-leased with D.M. Laurie, they were outmanoeuvred by the opportunism of two Tasmanians, G.H. Moore and R.Q. Kermode, who raised substantial capital to freehold the adjacent land at a price low enough to devalue their enterprise.[18] After this, Stoddart finally abandoned large pastoral lease-holding, probably without any significant increase in capital.

As early as 1852 he had purchased 50 acres freehold of the headland at Diamond Harbour and this was where he made his home. Over the next few years, he gradually added to his land. He accumulated another 311 acres from Crown grants and leased an additional 100 acres from the Church Property Trustees, so that, by 1862, he was farming over 450 acres.[19] Situated close to the port of Lyttelton, which provided a local market for produce, Diamond Harbour was ideal for a settled existence, and with his cousin, Mark Sprot, who had arrived in Canterbury in 1856, Stoddart cultivated the land, planted trees and established a garden and farm. Some time before his wedding he had a prefabricated cottage shipped out from Australia. This, located on a well-chosen site looking out across the bay and sheltered from the nor'-west and sou'-west winds, was where he and his wife raised their family.[20]

Between 1863 and 1872, Anna gave birth to seven children. The Stoddarts'

Stoddart's cottage, Diamond Harbour, 1980s.

Below: **Old Homestead, Diamond Harbour,** (c.1913)
Watercolour and bodycolour over charcoal
230 x 310mm
Private Collection

first child, named after his father, died when he was only two years old. Mark
Stoddart's diary entry on 26 May 1865, recorded simply: 'Poor Markie died at
home'. [21] Elizabeth Torlesse, who had been the boy's sponsor at his baptism,
arrived to stay with Anna on the following day, and the child was buried on
30 May at Holy Trinity, Lyttelton. The Stoddarts' eldest daughter, Frances, was
born in 1864, and named after Mark's older sister, an artist who lived in
Edinburgh. Margaret's arrival, on 3 October 1865, was noted by Mark in his
diary and underlined: 'No 3 born all well'. [22] She was baptised at Holy Trinity
on 1 November. Another son, James, followed in 1867, and Mary and Agnes
were born in 1868 and 1869. The youngest child, John, arrived in 1872.

On 10 March 1871, well-known Christchurch medical man and photographer Dr A.C. Barker visited the Stoddarts at Diamond Harbour with his
daughter Mary, [23] and his photograph of the couple in the garden with

Frances, Margaret and James presents a picture of plain but comfortable colonial living. Barker avoided the formality found in many portraits of this period, and his carefully posed yet casual grouping suggests the intimacy that existed between Margaret and her father. According to family tradition, the closeness between them dated back to her birth just over four months after the loss of his son.[24]

DIAMOND HARBOUR AND THE EXPERIENCE OF LANDSCAPE

Diamond Harbour, where Margaret Stoddart was born and where she spent her childhood, would become the subject for a succession of paintings in which she explored the bay's changing appearance under different moods and a variety of seasonal effects. Its sheltered harbour and wharf, the cottage she grew up in, and the gracious residence, known as Godley House, where she lived in later life with her mother and sisters, its flower garden and nearby blossom trees, provided artistic motifs that reflected her long and close relationship with the bays. The scenery around Diamond Harbour formed her first sensations of place, and a familiarity with this environment influenced the way that she related to the many differing European and New Zealand landscapes depicted in her painting. Any artist's representation of his or her surroundings is determined not only by landscape aesthetics but by a complex set of circumstances:[25] Margaret's geographic origins, and her emotional links to place, had an important bearing on her work.

Diamond Harbour is the open bay that lies between Purau and Charteris Bay on the south side of Lyttelton Harbour. Its Maori name is Te Waipapa but in 1857 it was known to settlers as 'Mr Stoddart's Bay'. According to Margaret it was her father, the first European resident, who named it Diamond Harbour on account of 'the glitter of the sun-track on the water, always very noticeable from that side of the harbour'.[26] The transformation of the Lyttelton bays by European settlement, which took place during her own lifetime, was fundamental to Margaret's experience of an evolving and changing landscape.

A View of Lyttelton Harbour from Governor's Bay, Banks Peninsula was one of fifteen colour plates of South Island sites published in 1877 in C.D. Barraud's viewbook, *New Zealand Graphic and Descriptive*, and the accompanying text reveals a contemporary fascination with the area's geological past and future development:

> The Peninsula consists of an extensive mass of volcanic mountains, the fires of which, however, have been extinct for ages. Lyttelton Harbour occupies one of the ancient craters, and, except at the entrance, where the cliffs do not exceed from two to three hundred feet in height, is surrounded by lofty hills, composed entirely of lava beds, ejected during the tremendous eruptions which occurred during the period of activity. The town of Lyttelton is built on a nook at the

C.D. Barraud, *A View of Lyttelton Harbour from Governors Bay, Banks Peninsula.*
New Zealand Graphic and Descriptive, 1877

Map of Banks Peninsula showing the various places where Margaret Stoddart and her family lived.

western side of the harbour, and presents a very picturesque appearance. Between it and the plains to the westward a line of railway has been constructed, the western wall of the volcano having been pierced by a tunnel nearly two miles long, an operation of great interest in a scientific as well as in a mercantile point of view.[27]

Colonisation changed the landscape – houses and farms gave the area a cultivated appearance, and grazing land and scattered planting encroached on the tussock of the brown hills. Patches of kowhai, ngaio and matipo survived in sheltered recesses and in 1861 the bays along the upper part of Lyttelton Harbour were regarded as providing 'some of the prettiest and best sites for residences in Canterbury'.[28] The process of turning land to productive use was vividly illustrated in the environment where Margaret Stoddart grew up. In 1861, an article in the *Lyttelton Times* singled out Mark Stoddart's property at Diamond Harbour as a picturesque feature in the Lyttelton landscape:

> The beauty of the spot, with the neat house, pretty garden and green fields about it, immediately arrest the eye; and the great extent of operations in progress, – nothing less than turning the whole foot of Mount Herbert into English pasture land, – indicates at once the ornament which the place will become to Port Cooper within the year now commencing.[29]

In 1858, with his cousin Mark Sprot, Stoddart had grown what was possibly the first crop of lucerne in New Zealand. A knowledge of plants was extremely important for the establishment of colonial settlement and his diary provides a record of the seasonal occupations that regulated the Stoddart family's existence when Margaret was a child. December and

January was the time for making blackcurrant jelly and strawberry jam, shearing the sheep and gathering up the hay for winter feed. The months from January to March were taken up with harvesting the fruit, which included plums, cherries, apricots, peaches, pears and apples. In April and May, they finished digging potatoes and began transplanting and laying out the garden. The winter months were for cutting down the gum trees for firewood, planting potatoes and transplanting fruit trees. In spring, they transplanted onions, and sowed carrots and parsnips.

Stoddart's diary included notes about stock, numbers of sheep killed, prices for produce and payment of wages, which appeared alongside records of family births, deaths, letters written to and received from Home, and visits to and from friends. There were numerous references to their neighbours, including Robert Heaton Rhodes, who lived at Purau from 1850 until 1866, and to Reginald Robert and Frances Bradley, who lived with their family at Charteris Bay. On Sundays, the Stoddarts attended church at Lyttelton and sometimes dined with Captain Frederick Henry Gibson, master of the port. The diary covered the years from 1862 until 1871, a period during which Mark and Anna kept in close touch with Elizabeth and Henry Torlesse and, on 9 October 1862, Mark recorded '3 pounds to Okains Bay C', a contribution to building St John the Evangelist's, which was completed in 1863.[30] By the time that the Torlesses moved from Okains Bay at the end of 1863, they had established a congregation, built a church, set up a school for children and organised both evening classes and a public library.[31]

There were also frequent trips to Ohinetahi at Governors Bay to see Thomas Potts, who arrived in the bays not long after Mark Stoddart and became one of his closest acquaintances. Potts had inherited £50,000 before emigrating to New Zealand with his wife, Emma, and their three sons, and in 1858 he purchased the property at Governors Bay from William Sefton Moorhouse. By 1867 he had transformed it into a large and impressive three-storeyed house, flanked by two wooden wings and a wide verandah. Ohinetahi became famous for its picturesque fernery and diversity of plants, and in the 1860s, Potts began laying out the garden, setting up irrigation channels, establishing a lawn, trellised arbours and flower beds. [32] Thomas and Emma Potts had a further ten children born in New Zealand, and their large family grew up at Ohinetahi.

Stoddart and Potts were interested in land management and they both served on the Canterbury Provincial Council, where Stoddart promoted his favourite project, the introduction of salmon to the province, and where Potts furthered the conservationist cause. Potts was an early advocate for the protection of native forests, arguing the case in Parliament and in an 1878 article published in the *New Zealand Country Journal*, in which he proposed the creation of national domains.[33] A noted naturalist and conservationist,

Church of St John the Evangelist, Okains Bay, Banks Peninsula, built in 1863.
Canterbury Museum, Christchurch

Thomas Henry Potts.
Canterbury Museum, Christchurch

in 1882 he put together a collection of essays, *Out in the Open*, one of the first substantial works on New Zealand's natural history that was published in this country.[34] In 1864, together with Julius von Haast and others, Stoddart and Potts founded the Canterbury Acclimatisation Society.[35]

Their association with Von Haast went back many years. Following Julius von Haast's marriage in 1863 to Mary Dobson, the newly-weds spent their honeymoon in what their son and his father's biographer Ferdinand von Haast later described as 'the crater of Lyttelton Harbour with [their] friends, the Potts's, and the Stoddarts under the combined auspices of Venus and Vulcan'.[36] In 1861, Von Haast had been appointed the geologist for the Canterbury Province and in 1868 he became the first director of the Canterbury Museum, one of the city's earliest cultural institutions, which played a significant role in the colonisation process. Under Von Haast's directorship, the museum was acknowledged to be one of the finest in Australasia, with an extensive herbarium of plant specimens, substantial holdings of rocks, minerals, fossils and skeletons, and a celebrated display on the moa, the flightless bird that Stoddart still believed to be in existence at the time of his first expedition into the hinterland, and which had aroused curiosity worldwide.[37] Von Haast also played an influential part in the development of art in the province, and he served with Potts on the Management Committee of the Canterbury Art Exhibition, which was held at the museum in 1870. This showed 365 paintings, including several works that had been lent by Margaret's father, and were painted by her aunt, Frances Stoddart, and uncle, Admiral James Stoddart.[38]

Julius von Haast at the Canterbury Museum, c. 1870.

Photo: Dr A.C. Barker. Canterbury Museum, Christchurch

Photograph of *River Scene* painted by Admiral Stoddart and shown at the Canterbury Art Exhibition, 1870.

Photo: Dr A.C. Barker. Canterbury Museum, Christchurch

The significance of background for female artists in this period is borne out clearly by Margaret's childhood. Her interests were shaped by her social origins and connections; she belonged to a family whose income and livelihood depended on the land, and whose position was tied into her father's identity as an explorer, early Canterbury runholder and farmer. Mark Stoddart's interest in natural history, angling and country sports, along with his attitude to land ownership and management, grew out of his background and his ambitions as a colonist. Margaret shared his enthusiasm for natural history and, through his connections, she gained useful introductions to some of the notable scientists in colonial society.

THE STODDARTS IN EDINBURGH

Four years after their marriage, Mark and Anna left with their children for Europe where they stayed in Scotland, and visited Anna's relations in Norway. Leaving Lyttelton on the *Himalaya* on 17 April 1866, they docked in London on 31 July, and caught the evening train to Edinburgh. The family remained in Scotland until the following year when they sailed on 6 June for Norway.[39] They embarked at Christiansand, and travelled to the capital, Christiania (as Oslo was then known), from where they made the 50-mile journey to Skien, described in a guidebook as 'one of the oldest municipal towns in the kingdom… the starting point of a journey through the grand district of Telemarken'.[40] Anna's father was a clergyman in the Episcopal Lutheran Church, who came originally from Skien. Mark Stoddart's diary records numerous names and places, presumably visits to relations, some of whom Margaret may have seen again when she came to Norway thirty years later as an artist, and painted at Fredricksroern and along the Christiania Fjord. Anna stayed on in Skien with the children until the end of July, before joining her husband in Edinburgh, and soon afterwards they sailed for New Zealand. Mark noted in his diary on 14 November 1867: 'Arrived by Glenmark, at home. Settled down again.'[41] Within five days of their homecoming, they were visited by Henry and Elizabeth Torlesse, and at the end of the week Mark went to call on Thomas Potts at Ohinetahi.

On 15 April 1876, Mark and Anna Stoddart and their family left Diamond Harbour once again for Scotland, sailing from Lyttelton on the *Jessie Osborne*. It was their second trip home in ten years, and this time the move was prompted by Mark Stoddart's failing health. About five years earlier, he had formed a trust and transferred his house and land to the trustees, Thomas Potts and Captain Gibson. The beneficiaries were himself and his wife, 'witnesseth that in consideration of the natural love which the said settler has for his wife the said Anna Barbara Stoddart and for other good and valuable consideration hereto moving…'[42] On 3 April 1876, about a week before their departure, the trustees sold the land, for £6,600, to Harvey

Hawkins, a Lyttelton merchant, and granted him a mortgage for the full sum. Interest was £400 per annum to be paid quarterly, and the capital was to be repaid in 1883. The establishment of the trust provided Mark Stoddart and his family with the security of a regular income for at least the next seven years.[43]

Under these circumstances the need to provide for their children's education may well have seemed more urgent to both parents. Anna, who had been forced by her husband's illness to organise their departure, expressed, in a letter written to William Allan of Diamond Harbour, the deep regret that she had felt on leaving New Zealand:

> Many many times we spoke about you and I never felt so sorry as I did to leave New Zealand this time. However I am thankful to say Mr Stoddart improved in health very much on the voyage and is now well and strong but his eyesight I fear will not be better. He consulted the best oculist here Dr Argyle Robertson whose opinion agrees with Dr Hay's – he can see no sign of cataract and says it is nervous entirely… Edinburgh is a wonderful city abounding in schools and the most splendid buildings of all kinds – the traffic is perfectly wonderful – tramway cars running in all directions… My brother wishes us to settle at Dover but Mr Stoddart I think will prefer Edinburgh – I would not mind going back to N.Z. tomorrow… I am always thinking of you all – if I could only have got the children to school I would never have parted with D.H.[44]

After settling her family into a new house and enrolling her children at school, Anna reflected on the change in their situation, in a later letter to William Allan:

> Many thanks for your kind long entertaining letters so interesting to us. We received yours of July 28 and very much enjoyed hearing of all your doings. My heart is in the old place [Diamond Harbour] altho' as it was I feel we did right not being able to work it like an active man with capital at his command. It will be a beautiful place. Since we left the ship I have really had hard work to get ourselves settled with all the children at home. Now however I think we are so far snug for the winter which is coming on – the schools are commencing in a fortnight and we have enrolled Jim in Stewart's Hospital which now belongs to the Merchant Co & two eldest girls in the Merchant Maiden School in Queen St. They will have quite two miles to walk each way but other children go from our neighbourhood & in the very bad weather they can go by tramway. Well sometimes I feel so sorry at having parted from D.H. but still as it was I could not help myself – one thing I believe that in a few years time all being well we will be out again and settle down for good. In the meantime I trust Mr Stoddart and the children will have benefited – Mr S always says it saved his life – anyway I feel I have done what I could for him…[45]

Margaret studied at the college for just over two years, won a bursary and prizes, and may have received some of her first drawing lessons from the art master, James Coutts.[46] She also made contact with her origins.

Margaret's family traced their ancestry back to the fifteenth century when they were landowners on the Scottish borders,[47] and her immediate forebears were raised in Edinburgh towards the close of its classical age, when the city was a centre of intellectual life. They had inherited something of its cultural traditions and gained some modest distinction themselves in artistic and literary fields. Her uncle, Thomas Tod Stoddart, lived at the border town of Kelso where he pursued his interest in angling and in writing poetry, activities that won him minor fame among his contemporaries.[48] Her uncle, Admiral James Stoddart, was a watercolourist who had shown at the Royal Scottish Academy, and her aunt, Frances Stoddart, was a noted Edinburgh artist.[49] Like her more famous contemporaries, the Nasmyth sisters, Frances specialised in landscape painting, which was considered a suitable genre for women artists. Evidently a woman of means, she painted at many popular mid-Victorian locations in England and Scotland as well as on the continent, where she toured the Alps and Italian lakes.[50] Frances was twenty-one years old when she made her debut at the Royal Academy, London and between 1863 and 1867 she exhibited no fewer than 110 works at the Royal Scottish Academy. She also exhibited in London at the first exhibition of the Society of Female Artists in 1857, and for the next four years.

Bellevue Terrace, Edinburgh, where Frances Stoddart lived between 1838 and 1861, is situated in a part of the New Town built in the 1820s and 1830s.

Frances evidently enjoyed some popularity; she gained favourable reviews in *The Scotsman* and was ranked twelfth in a list of over 105 female artists who were patronised by the Art Union prize winners in the Victorian period.[51] Margaret was only a child when Frances died but her example probably played some part in conditioning her later artistic ambitions.[52] Frances's painting was admired greatly in the Stoddart family circle in New Zealand, where she was known to a friend, Edward Chudleigh, as 'Miss Stoddart R.A.'.[53]

THE CANTERBURY COLLEGE SCHOOL OF ART, CHRISTCHURCH

The Stoddarts returned to New Zealand in 1879. Travelling as saloon passengers on *The Crusader*, they arrived at Lyttelton on 24 September. In all, they had spent about three years away during what was a formative period in Margaret's development. With the help of a substantial mortgage from Mark's brother, James, they moved to Fendalton in Christchurch, and in 1880 they settled into a spacious two-storeyed house which they had built and named Lismore Lodge after Lismore Island in Scotland. A comfortable and solid home, with a verandah marking the main entrance, it was set back from the road in its own grounds. Margaret was to have her first studio space here in the south- and east-facing room.[54]

The Stoddarts realised the importance of education for women, and in Edinburgh they had provided not only for their son's schooling but for that of his two older sisters as well. Back in New Zealand they also encouraged

Lismore Lodge, Fendalton.

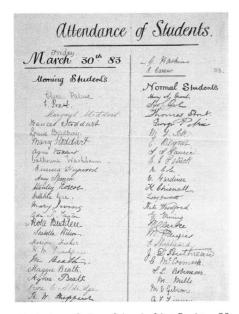

Canterbury College School of Art Register, 30 March 1883, which includes the signatures of the Stoddart sisters, Margaret, Frances, Agnes and Mary, and Kate Sheppard.

Canterbury College School of Art.

their children's studies: James and John attended Christ's College, and Margaret and Frances were enrolled with their younger sisters, Mary and Agnes, at the Canterbury College School of Art in its opening year, 1882.[55]

The school's principal function was to instruct students in drawing, designing and modelling for the development of trades and manufacturing in the colony, and to provide schoolteachers with art training and drawing skills. Its classes were based on the model of art education devised by the Department of Science and Art at South Kensington, and under its head-master, David Blair (1850-1925), and its principal teacher, George Herbert Elliott (1860-1941), both of whom had trained in England under this system, it also provided basic instruction in painting in oil and watercolours.[56] At the morning class attended by Margaret and her sisters in 1882, at least thirty-eight out of forty-three students were female and, at a £4 yearly fee, double the cost of the evening courses, it catered mainly for middle-class women.[57] No doubt some students were content to cultivate traditional feminine accomplishments but the significance of the school in providing this gener-ation of female students with a training to work in teaching and art and design should not be underestimated.[58]

In the first ten years, twenty-five out of fifty-two students who gained a teaching qualification, the Full Second Grade or Art Students Certificate, were women, and included Margaret and Frances.[59] Edith Munnings (1867-1939) and Rosa Budden (later Sawtell) (1865-1940), one of Margaret's lifelong friends, both found junior positions at the school. Many female students went on to teach, including Helen Gibson, the founder in 1889 of a girls' school later to become known as Rangi Ruru.[60] Margaret Stoddart and Dora Meeson (1869-1955) were the school's earliest professional artists; Margaret's attendance, from 1882 until 1884 and then from 1887 until the end of 1890, overlapped with Dora's, and their time together as students and later as expatriate artists in England made this a significant association in a period when relationships between women artists frequently reinforced their ambitions. Dora Meeson attended the Canterbury School of Art from 1888 until 1890,[61] before studying at the National Gallery School in Melbourne, the Slade School of Art in London from 1896 to 1898, and, from 1898 to 1899, at the Académie Julian in Paris. She remained in England, where she painted professionally and became an ardent campaigner for women's franchise.[62]

With the foundation of the school in 1882, and of the Canterbury Society of Arts two years earlier, art began to play a larger part in the life of middle-class Christchurch. Regarded in late colonial society as an important cultural and civilising influence, art was an area in which women participated from the beginning. In the 1880s, just under half the exhibiting members of the Canterbury Society of Arts were female and in 1885 Margaret became a member of its council.[63] At this time the distinction between amateur and professional was not clear-cut, and women worked in a local context, free of restrictive practices imposed by professional organisations. Their participation in art often provided a useful addition to a family's income and a way for middle-class women to achieve some independence without compromising their social position.

There is every reason to suppose that, at first, Margaret saw painting as a discreet source of income. In 1886, Frances Hodgkins's sister Isabel (later Field) received £50 from the sale of her paintings and, only two years later, she travelled to the Centennial Exhibition in Melbourne on earnings of £79.[64] In 1892, the cash book of the Canterbury Society of Arts recorded that Margaret's sales came to 19 guineas, which compared favourably with Isabel's in Christchurch that year, which were around £18. Between 1892 and 1897, Margaret averaged £16 a year.[65] She also had additional income from commissions, private sales and presumably from works that she sent regularly to art society exhibitions around the country. One measure of her success is the recognition she received early on from the Canterbury Society of Arts, which, in 1885, acquired *A Mountain Lily* at £5 5s and *Roses* at £3 10s for its permanent collection.[66] In 1887, the Canterbury Museum purchased two paintings for £5 and twelve drawings of New Zealand flowers for £6 6s in 1890.[67]

Family circumstances also underline the usefulness of Margaret's earnings around this time. Mark Stoddart had been unable to work since 1876, and he died on 28 August 1885. The probate record showed a bank balance of under £53, which did not cover his funeral and medical expenses of over £64, and combined clothing and grocery bills of just over £10. Anna also inherited the mortgage for £1,790 that Mark had taken out with his brother, James, although a family arrangement meant this was not discharged until many years later. The Stoddarts lived on the income from the trust, which had sold the Diamond Harbour estate to Harvey Hawkins. Hawkins's failure to discharge the principal in 1883, and an extension of his mortgage by the trust, meant that the family were provided for after Mark's death. But, although Anna and her children were well taken care of, it was clear that the older ones needed to support themselves in adult life.[68]

During the late nineteenth century, changes in material circumstances and social structures caused many women to gradually redefine their place in society. The transformation of New Zealand from a frontier to a modern society gave Margaret and Frances Stoddart an opportunity to gain an education and professional qualifications that brought them more options and greater independence. Women in New Zealand had equal entry to art schools and universities from the beginning and, as 'the first Australasian town in which university education for women took full root',[69] Christchurch

Silver medal awarded to Margaret Stoddart by the Auckland Society of Arts for Best Work in Class 2, 1886.

Bronze Medal awarded to Margaret Stoddart by the Auckland Society of Arts for Class IV. Sec. XVII, 1888. Both medals were designed by Anton Teutenberg and feature New Zealand flora.

Canterbury Museum, Christchurch

had a high record of female graduates. Margaret, and her sister Frances, who gained a BA degree in 1893,[70] were both young women with proven abilities and their family background goes a long way towards explaining their direction.

Anna Stoddart was an educated woman who had assumed increasing responsibility for her family from the onset of her husband's illness in the mid-1870s. Edward Chudleigh, who was a regular visitor to the Stoddarts' home in the 1880s, described her as a 'clever woman', and acknowledged the part she had played in the upbringing of her girls, whom he admired 'as fine and clever as well'.[71] But, despite these remarks, Chudleigh still maintained what were then widely held views on the role of women in colonial society; he noted with some satisfaction that Frances's education had made no difference to her true sense of female obligation:

> Looked up George Draper. Dr and Mrs Harvey. Walter Empson and Agnes and Miss Stoddart, our Marjory's [*sic*] eldest sister and a right good girl. She is a splendid woman full of learning and strength and yet quite a woman, ready to sink all things to her home and woman's duties. I was as much taken with her as with Maggie and the two younger girls. The old lady must have had a lot of good in her to bring up her girls so well. Such fine ladies and clear good brains.[72]

Chudleigh's comment hints at the disapproval many women faced when they attempted to pursue a career while social pressures still discouraged such a move, lest it encroach upon what was seen as their traditional role, defined by Thomas Bracken in 1887 as 'the light of the home and genius of the fireside'.[73]

In the late 1880s and 1890s, women's place in society became increasingly the subject for debate as middle-class women became involved in the suffrage campaign and in a range of issues related to social justice and civil rights. On 19 September 1893, the Electoral Act was passed, granting New Zealand women the right to vote in parliamentary elections.[74] Margaret's position on the matter remains unclear. Her response to the event, made privately in a letter to her friend, Rosa Dixon, revealed her sharp sense of humour, directed, on this occasion, at the opportunism of political life:

> Have you been to register your vote yet? We are all flocking to do so here even the most determined opponents of woman's franchise are taking their womenkind off to register their votes, of course they say in self defence. I wonder if it was an immediate result of the franchise, that this morning we got the most beautiful smile and wave of his hat from the candidate for the Riccarton Electorate. We don't know him and he never did such a thing before but we stood up two inches more on the spot.[75]

She continued in the same ironical tone: 'I am beginning to think now that it is right that women should have a voice in the state, and on polling days some delightful drag parties might be arranged. Don't think me very flippant, but I am freshening up after yesterday's walk.'[76] Margaret was acquainted with one of the leaders of the campaign, Kate Sheppard, who attended numerous early classes with the Stoddart sisters at the School of Art,[77] but the only member of her family to have signed the 1893 suffrage petition was her sister, Frances. Margaret's fellow students at the School of Art, Edith Munnings and Dora Meeson, were also signatories but the absence of her name leaves open what specific significance the franchise movement had for her then.

In 1889, Margaret gained the Second Grade Full Certificate, and in 1890, at the age of twenty-five, she completed her studies at the school. While women's participation in art was still seen predominantly as an accomplishment, she progressed towards professional practice discreetly by working in the genteel area of flower painting.

NOTES:

1. Anne Kirker, 'Towards a Professional Status', in *New Zealand Women Artists: a survey of 150 years*, rev. ed., East Roseville, NSW, 1993, pp.24-42.

2. Victoria Hammond and Juliet Peers, *Completing the Picture: women artists and the Heidelberg era*, Hawthorn, East Victoria, 1992; Jane Hyslton, *South Australian Women Artists: paintings from the 1890s to the 1940s*, Ex. Cat. Art Gallery of South Australia, Adelaide, 1994; Maria Tippett, *By a Lady: celebrating three centuries of art by Canadian women*, Toronto, 1992; Patricia Trenton, ed., *Independent Spirits: women painters of the American West, 1890-1945*, Ex. Cat. Autry Museum of Western Heritage, Berkeley, c.1995.

3. Ann Schjotte, Ann 23 Governess Down *Matoaka*. Assisted Emigration to Canterbury, New Zealand by the ship *Matoaka* 2 December 1860, Shipping Passenger List Micro 465, Canterbury Museum, Christchurch. Her age, like the spelling of her name, was probably recorded incorrectly. In Nina Jones's Birthday Album, Anna's date of birth was given as 1835. Her death certificate on 6 June 1911 recorded her age as seventy-six.

4. Charlotte Macdonald, *A Woman of Good Character: single women as immigrant settlers in New Zealand*, Wellington, 1990, p.4.

5. Notes opposite entry, 5 August 1887, E.C. Richards, *Diary of E.R. Chudleigh 1862-1921*, Macmillan Brown Library, University of Canterbury, Christchurch.

6. The journey is described in W. Herbert Allington Diary 28 August-26 December 1860, Canterbury Museum, Christchurch; the SS *Matoaka*'s arrival is recorded in the *Lyttelton Times*, 5 December 1860.

7. Charlotte Julia Doratea Weale was also remembered in Northland as Mihi Wira, on account of her intervention in the tour of England by a party of Maori organised by William Jenkins in 1863. According to Brian Mackrell, she was then the superintendent of a girls' home in Birmingham, and 'a strong-willed woman of considerable means, with an influential circle of friends including Bishop Selwyn…' Brian Mackrell, *Hariru Wikitoria: An illustrated history of the Maori tour of England, 1863*, Auckland, 1985, p.85. Doratea Weale made numerous benefactions to Northland Maori churches, Mackrell, p. 103, and R.M. Ross, 'The Maori Church in Northland', in Historic Places Trust, *Historic Buildings in New Zealand North Island*. Also, Mark Pringle Stoddart (1819-1885) Macdonald Dictionary of Canterbury Biographies, Canterbury Museum, Christchurch. Frances Torlesse added that, after Doratea Weale's return to England, '…for the rest of her life [she] never ceased her prayers for the best welfare of the church in Canterbury and gave her influence and her money to further the work which was afterwards attempted'. From a letter dictated by Frances Torlesse to Edith (Miss Mellish) of Christchurch, 16 October 1920. Canterbury Museum, Christchurch.

8. Gordon Ogilvie, *Banks Peninsula: Cradle of Canterbury*, Wellington, 1990, p. 119.

9. For information about Elizabeth, see Jo-Anne Smith, 'Elizabeth Torlesse', *The Book of New Zealand Women Ko Kui Ma Te Kaupapa*, Wellington, 1991; Jo-Anne Smith, 'Elizabeth Torlesse', *The Dictionary of New Zealand Biography, Vol.1 1769-1869*, Wellington, 1990.

10. Elizabeth Henrietta Torlesse, Reminiscences of early Canterbury and about the Revell Family 1853-1920s, Folder 344, pp.5-6. Canterbury Museum, Christchurch.

11. *Ibid*.

12. Edward Merson Templar (1820-1897) and Mark Pringle Stoddart (1819-1885) Macdonald

Dictionary of Canterbury Biographies, Canterbury Museum, Christchurch; Mark P. Stoddart, Reminiscences, Canterbury Museum, Christchurch.

13. L.G.D. Acland, *The Early Canterbury Runs*, 4th ed., Christchurch, 1975, p.94.

14. W. David McIntyre, ed., *The Journal of Henry Sewell 1853-7*, Vol. I, Christchurch, 1980, pp.196-197.

15. Charlotte Godley, *Letters from Early New Zealand by Charlotte Godley 1850-1853*, Christchurch, 1951, pp.317-18.

16. McIntyre, ed., *The Journal of Henry Sewell 1853-57*, Vol. I, p.176.

17. Letter of acceptance, 2 February 1853, General Assembly Library, cited in Mark Pringle Stoddart (1819-1885), Macdonald Dictionary of Canterbury Biographies, Canterbury Museum; Acland, *The Early Canterbury Runs*, p.94.

18. Acland, pp. 275-276; W.J. Gardner, ed., *A History of Canterbury*, Vol.II, Christchurch, 1971, p. 37.

19. In the Diamond Harbour area he owned: RS 246 Area 50 acres. Purchased for £150 from the Canterbury Association on 14.08.52 [4D 242]; RS 1333 Crown grant on 01.06.59. size 173 acres [18D 80]; RS 498 Crown grant on 07.07.60. size 80 acres [18D 81]; RS 2404 Crown grant on 22.10.62. size 58 acres [22.10.62]. In addition, he leased RS 234e (100 acres) from the Church Property Trustees on 04.09.58 for a twenty-one-year term, the yearly rent £25 [18D 79]. I am indebted to John Wilson for this research.

20. Stoddart's cottage is the oldest house in Diamond Harbour and an excellent example of colonial prefabrication, made out of Australian hardwood with a slate roof. Dr Miles Lewis has, however, recently suggested that the cottage may have originally come from Europe or California, and was imported to Australia to provide housing during the gold rushes of the 1850s. It has been carefully restored by the Friends of Stoddart's Cottage. I am grateful to the Historic Places Trust for this information.

21. 26 May 1865, M.P. Stoddart Diary 1862-1871, Micro MS 24, Alexander Turnbull Library, National Library of New Zealand.

22. 3 October 1865, M.P. Stoddart Diary 1862-1871; 'Margaret Olrog' probably came from her mother's side of the family. At Mary's baptism in 1868, Margaret Schjött, presumably a relative, was recorded as the child's sponsor. In 1869, Ernestine Schjött, acted as Agnes's sponsor.

23. 'Dr Barker and Mary here taking Photos'. 10 March 1871, M.P. Stoddart Diary 1862-1871.

24. Mrs Frances Dainty in conversation with the author, June 1984.

25. Petra ten-Doesschate Chu, 'It Took Millions of Years to Compose That Picture', in Sarah Faunce and Linda Courbet, eds, *Courbet Reconsidered*, Ex. Cat., Brooklyn Museum, NY, 1988, pp.55-65.

26. J.C. Andersen, *Place Names of Banks Peninsula*, Wellington, 1927, p.61. Mary Stapylton-Smith, *Diamond Harbour: Portrait of a Community*, Diamond Harbour, 1993.

27. W.T.L. Travers, ed., with illustrations by C.D. Barraud, *New Zealand Graphic and Descriptive*, London, 1877, p.29.

28. 'At the upper part of Lyttelton Harbour are bays where dairy farming, gardening, and general agriculture are pursued with great success. Here are some of the prettiest and best sites for residences in Canterbury, and from these spots the town of Lyttelton is supplied with the greater part of its requirements in connection with the farm and garden.' *Lyttelton Times*, 5 January 1861, p.4; H.C. Jacobson, *Tales of Banks Peninsula*, 3rd ed., 1914, p.318.

29. *Lyttelton Times*, 5 January 1861, p.4.

30. 9 October 1862, M.P. Stoddart Diary 1862-1871.

31. Stephen Parr, *Canterbury Pilgrimage: the first hundred years of the Church of England in Canterbury New Zealand*, Christchurch, 1951, pp.88-89; Gordon Ogilvie, *Banks Peninsula: Cradle of Canterbury*. Henry Torlesse subsequently took on the chaplaincy of the hospital, gaol and Sunnyside Lunatic Asylum in Christchurch; he also acted as chaplain to the House of Female Refuge which he and Elizabeth had established, and she looked after. Their friendship with the Stoddarts continued and on 2 June 1864 the *Lyttelton Times* recorded that Mrs Stoddart had collected £9 towards the female refuge. Ill health forced Henry's resignation in 1867. In June, he was appointed the vicar at Governors Bay, but died only three years later, leaving his wife with seven young children to support.

32. Joseph Munnings described Ohinetahi in December, 1863: 'Water laid on from a gully up the hill, to within a few yards of the back door, garden nicely laid out, & even now looks beautiful although most of the flowers have done blooming. 2 arbours of trellace [sic] work, choice creepers planted around in a few years will be very nice place.' The Diaries of Joseph Munnings (1841-1923), Canterbury Museum, 21 December, 1863, quoted by Jo-Anne Smith, 'The early days of Ohinetahi', *Press*, 10 January 1991.

33. T.H. Potts, 'National Domains', *New Zealand Country Journal*, Vol. II, No.4, July 1878, pp.227-233; Paul Star, Thomas Henry Potts, *The Dictionary of New Zealand Biography*, Vol. 2 1870-1900, Wellington, 1993.

34. T.H. Potts, *Out in the Open: a budget of scraps of natural history gathered in New Zealand*, Christchurch, 1882.

35. R.M. McDowall, *Gamekeepers for the Nation: the story of New Zealand's acclimatisation societies 1861-1990*, Christchurch, 1994, p.22.

36. H.F. von Haast, *The Life and Times of Julius von Haast, Explorer, Geologist, Museum Builder*, Wellington, 1948, p.1068.

37. Mark P. Stoddart Reminiscences, Canterbury Museum, Christchurch; McIntyre, ed., *The Journal of Henry Sewell 1853-57*, Vol.I, p.308.

38. The exhibition included two oil paintings by Miss Stoddart lent by Mr M.P. Stoddart: 17, *Glen Lyn, Perthshire* and 92, *Mount Hutt, from the Rakaia*. (This raises the question of a possible visit by Frances Stoddart to New Zealand, although the painting may have been executed in Scotland from a sketch.) 109, *View on the Tummell, in Perthshire* was exhibited by Mr R Waitt. Two watercolours by Admiral Stoddart were lent by Mr M.P. Stoddart: 49, *River-scene* and 135, *Ship in a Storm*. For the Canterbury Art Exhibition, Neil Roberts, *A Canterbury Perspective, Nga Taonga Titiro Whakamuri i Roto i Waitaha, Amateurs and Itinerants: Art in Canterbury 1840-1890*, Robert McDougall Art Gallery, Christchurch, 1990.

39. 6 June 1866, M.P. Stoddart Diary 1862-1871.

40. *Handbook for Travellers in Norway*, John Murray, London, 1897, p.35; 'The clergy, speaking generally, are a well-educated class of men, many of them being acquainted with the literature of Europe and familiar with standard works in the German and English languages', p.24.

41. 14 November 1867, M.P. Stoddart Diary 1862-1871.

42. The trust was formed on 13 June 1871 [56D 17].

43. The date of sale was 3 April 1876 [73D 775]; the trustees granted a mortgage on the same day [73D 771].

44. Typescript of letter from Anna Stoddart to William Allan, Diamond Harbour, Lyttelton, Canterbury, New Zealand from 65 Frederick Street, Edinburgh, 27 July 1876. I would like to acknowledge the generosity of Mr Allan Taylor in making these letters available.

45. Typescript of letter from Anna Stoddart to William Allan, Diamond Harbour, Lyttelton, Canterbury, New Zealand, from Ellerslie Villa, Colt Bridge Terrace, Edinburgh, 14 September 1876.

46. Margaret's enrolment, No. 3267, is recorded in 1876 in the register of the Edinburgh Ladies College, now known as the Mary Erskine School. Ruth Burgess, Margaret O. Stoddart (1865-1934), 1985, p.18, Canterbury Public Library, Christchurch.

47. 'The Late Mr Thomas Tod Stoddart', *Kelso Chronicle*, 26 November 1880. Stoddart Papers, Canterbury Museum, Christchurch.

48. 'The Late Mr T.T. Stoddart', *Illustrated London News*, 11 December 1880, p.573, Stoddart papers, Canterbury Museum, Christchurch; Margaret's cousin, Anna Stoddart, who was the daughter of Thomas Tod Stoddart, was a writer. She published at least nine books, including a biography of the Victorian traveller, Isabella Bird, *The Life of Isabella Bird – Mrs Bishop*, London, 1906. Anna M. Stoddart, *British Museum General Catalogue of Printed Books*, London, 1964.

49. James Stoddart exhibited four marine paintings at the Royal Scottish Academy in 1839.

50. At her first exhibition at the Royal Scottish Academy in 1838 she showed: 3, *View near the lake of Brientz*, 292, *Loch Katrine*, 310, *Valley of the Lauterbrunnen*. The picturesque sites where she worked in Britain included the Borders, along the Tay, at Sutherland in the north, Skye and the English Lakes.

51. Pamela Gerrish Nunn, *Victorian Women Artists*, London, 1987, p.115; 'Miss Stoddart advances with laudable industry in her profession. She exhibits this year no fewer than six paintings, not crudely dashed off but elaborated with obvious care… *Head of Loch Lomond* (No. 289), is, if we mistake it not, Miss Stoddart's largest painting, and shows considerable vigour of style with a pleasing unity of effect. The rocky knoll in middle-distance, although fashioned after Macculloch, is really executed in a high style of art', *The Scotsman*, 26 March 1842, p.3. Despite Frances's popularity no works have been located in public collections, although her painting, *Bonting Bridge*, was sold through Christie's at Phillips, Ipswich, in December 1993 for US$1, 267.

52. Frances Stoddart died 22 May 1867 at 43 Heriot Row, Edinburgh, *Edinburgh Evening Courant*, 23 May 1867, p. 4.

53. Reginald Chudleigh: '…at Geoffs, I saw a splendid oil painting called, I believe On the Tunny. It was I found, painted by Marjory [sic] Stoddart's aunt a Miss Stoddart R.A. It was a very well known picture. Mr Stoddart was often pressed to sell it by Mr Waite [sic]… One day Mr Stoddart and Mr Waite [sic] bet one valued thing against another. Mr Stoddart lost, and lost this picture to his lasting sorrow. All he asked was that Mr and Mrs Waite [sic] would call it a gift and a wedding present.' E.C. Richards, 5 August, 1887, *Diary of E.R. Chudleigh 1862-1921*.

54. The land was purchased on 19 September 1880 for £540 [Transfer 13421] with a mortgage for £1790 from Admiral James Stoddart of Queens Gardens, Hyde Park, London [M 10285].

It was sold to Professor Arnold Wall in 1902, and his son, also named Arnold, recalled that the artist's studio was the south- and east-facing room. Arnold Wall Letter File TL 3/1/1/, 3 November 1983, Alexander Turnbull Library, National Library.

55. Canterbury College School of Art Roll, 1882, School of Fine Arts, University of Canterbury, Christchurch.

56. The school was established to develop 'the application of Art to the common uses of life, and to the requirements of Trade and Manufactures' and it offered instruction in a range of subjects, including Machine Construction and Building Construction, Modelling, Illustration, Design for the manufacture of furniture, carpets, tiles, ceilings etc. *School of Art Canterbury College Prospectus*, 1882, School of Fine Arts, University of Canterbury; F. Graeme Chalmers, 'South Kensington and the Colonies: David Blair of New Zealand and Canada', *Studies in Art Education*, Vol. 26, No. 2, Winter 1985, pp.69-74.

57. Second Term, 1882, Canterbury College School of Art Roll.

58. Ann Calhoun, 'A Trade for their Daughters: Women in the fine and applied arts in New Zealand from 1870 to 1900', *Bulletin of New Zealand Art History*, Vol. 14, 1993, pp.15-28.

59. *School of Art Canterbury College Prospectus*, 1894.

60. Margaret Belcher, *A History of Rangi-Ruru School*, Christchurch, n.d., p.18.

61. Canterbury College School of Art Roll, 1888-1890.

62. Myra Scott, 'Dora Meeson Coates', in Joan Kerr, ed., *Heritage: The National Women's Art Book*, Roseville East, 1995.

63. 22 September 1885, Canterbury Society of Arts Minute Book, Robert McDougall Art Gallery, Christchurch.

64. E.H. McCormick, W*orks of Frances Hodgkins in New Zealand*, Auckland, 1954, p.15.

65. 1892-1897, Canterbury Society of Arts Cash Book, Canterbury Society of Arts, Christchurch.

66. Julie King, 'Art Collecting by the Canterbury Society of Arts: The First Fifty Years', *Bulletin of New Zealand Art History*, Vol. II, 1990, pp.41-50.

67. 28 November 1887; 23 December 1889; 17 March 1890, Museum Committee Minutes, Records, University of Canterbury.

68. Probate Mark Pringle Stoddart, National Archives, Christchurch; Mortgage between Mark Pringle Stoddart and James Stoddart [M 10285]. When he was around twenty years old, Margaret's brother James left New Zealand in 1887 for Africa, where he served in the army, and was killed at Bulawayo in 1901. John followed his brother and fought in Africa but established himself as a cattle rancher in Rhodesia, where he died unmarried in 1926. 'The Christ's College register April 1897 Old Boys and Masters', S.D. Barker, Newspaper Cuttings Vol. II, 1896-97, Canterbury Museum, Christchurch. Agnes and Mary remained at home and cared for their mother until Mary married in 1908.

69. W.J. Gardner, *Colonial Cap and Gown*, University of Canterbury, Christchurch, p.72 and p.106.

70. Frances Stoddart taught from 1890 to 1891 at Christchurch Girls' High School. Barbara Peddie, *Christchurch Girls' High School 1877-1977*, Christchurch High School Old Girls' Association, Christchurch, 1977. I am grateful to Vickie Hearnshaw for this reference.

71. E.C. Richards, 20 June 1887, *Diary of E.R. Chudleigh 1862-1921.*

72. *Ibid.*, 5 August 1887.

73. Quoted by Raewyn Dalziel, in 'The Colonial Helpmeet. Women's Role and the Vote in Nineteenth-Century New Zealand', *New Zealand Journal of History*, Vol. II, No.2, October 1977, pp.112-123.

74. Judith Devaliant, *Kate Sheppard: The Fight for Women's Votes in New Zealand*, Auckland, 1992; Margaret Lovell-Smith, *How Women Won the Vote – A Canterbury Perspective*, Canterbury Museum, Christchurch, 1993. Some of the different interpretations of the significance and social consequences for women from the franchise and the WCTU campaign are summarised in Erik Olssen and Marcia Stenson, *A Century of Change New Zealand 1800-1900*, Auckland, 1994, pp.373-388.

75. Letter to Rosa Dixon from Margaret Stoddart, Fendalton, 24 September 1893. Private Collection. I would like to acknowledge the generosity of Mr Marmaduke Spencer Bower in making these letters available.

76. *Ibid.*

77. Kate Sheppard enrolled at the art school in 1882 with her sister Marie Beath, and her two nieces, Agnes and Margaret. I am grateful to Tessa Malcolm and Margaret Lovell-Smith for confirming Kate Sheppard's signature in the register.

THE MAKING OF A FLOWER PAINTER

FLOWERS AND FEMININITY

Margaret Stoddart's initial direction and achievements as an artist were shaped by ideas about gender that associated flower painting with femininity, and by the widespread colonial interest in indigenous flora, which gave her an incentive to explore the landscape in search of plant specimens.

Her style was formed by the teaching she received at the Canterbury College School of Art, which emphasised close observation and truth to nature. The tuition was based on South Kensington's disciplined structure, with students proceeding systematically through strictly defined stages of instruction. Training began with perspective drawing using geometrical instruments, and progressed to working freehand from the flat (using prints and drawings), and from the model (using geometrical models, vases and household objects, plaster casts etc). The teaching emphasised accuracy and students learned to draw what they saw faithfully in precise outlines, and to register three dimensions tonally through light and shade. At the end of the year, Margaret gained a pass in freehand and in model drawing and, at the exhibition of students' work, she was represented by a study of ivy leaves drawn in sepia from the cast, and by several watercolour drawings of flowers.[1]

Botanical drawing and flower painting was one of the subjects taught at the school, and fresh specimens of a plant in flower were examined in weekly lectures on Friday mornings. Students were taught to identify botanical characteristics and draw them in detail, giving close attention to each individual part – stem, leaves, stalk, stipules, spines and tendrils, flower buds, flower parts and fruit. The results of Margaret's training are seen in the accuracy of her representation in *Titoki Berries*, 1886, a study painted against a conventional plain ground, in *Mandevilla*, 1888, where the plant is depicted growing in situ, and in early still-life paintings of floral arrangements such as *Cherry Blossom*, 1890. The inclusion of botanical art in the school's curriculum was related to its application to design and it also reflected the value this period placed on recording natural phenomena.

In 1883, when Margaret was seventeen years old, she made her debut at the Annual Exhibition of the Canterbury Society of Arts with a variety of floral subjects, including roses, arum lilies and native daisies, painted on panels and terracotta plaques.[2] The popularity of flower painting among female painters in Canterbury may have originated partly from the school's botanical classes. Floral screens, ornamental plates, along with a large and varied assortment of flower pictures painted on panels, terracotta, silk and satin, made a regular appearance at art shows where they fitted within the tradition of the female amateur. Neither regarded as art, nor collected by

COURSES OF STUDY.

Before proceeding to definite courses of study, students are required to take up ELEMENTARY DRAWING or show evidence that they have already done so, it comprises :—

Stages III. *a.*, IV. *a.* Freehand from flat examples, blackboard lessons.
  I. *a., b.* Elementary Geometry, plane and solid, 12 lectures.
  I. *c.* Perspective, parallel and angular, 12 lectures.
  III. *b.* Drawing from models, blackboard lessons.

In following out the courses of instruction, students are required to pass in the following stages.

COURSE I.—FOR STUDENTS WISHING TO STUDY FLOWERS, STILL-LIFE AND LANDSCAPE.

Stage IV. *b.* Outlining ornament from the round.
  III. *c.*, IV. *c.* Shading from the flat.
  II. *c.* Advanced perspective.
  V. *a., b.* Foliage in outline. Lectures on plant form.
  VI. *a., b.* Landscape from the flat.
  III. *d.*, IV. *d.* Shading from the round.
  V. *c., d.* Flower painting.
  VI. *c., d.* Landscape and still-life.

Students at the Canterbury College School of Art were required to complete elementary drawing before taking one of the courses of study. Initially Margaret took Course 1: Flowers, Still life and Landscape.
Canterbury College School of Art Prospectus, 1882

Lectures on botany and plant form took place on Friday morning.
Canterbury College School of Art Prospectus, 1882

BOTANY AND PLANT FORM.

Every Friday morning at 11 o'clock, students who are working in Stage V. will attend a short lecture on Botanical Drawing and Plant Form as applied to Art. Fresh specimens of a plant then in flower will be supplied at each lecture for the use of students; it will be drawn in detail on the blackboard; its botanical characteristics pointed out, with suggestions for ornamental arrangement.

The position of the plant in the vegetable kingdom.
The stem; its form and branching.
Form of the leaves; the stalk and its insertion, stipules, spines and tendrils.
The leaf and flower bud.
The fully expanded flower and its parts; the fruit.
The plant applied to design.

Alectryon excelsum (Titoki), 1886
Watercolour and bodycolour over traces of pencil on dull
green paper
355 x 270mm
Canterbury Museum, Christchurch

Mandevilla, 1888
Watercolour and bodycolour
470 x 310mm
Collection of Justin Hobbs, Esq.

galleries, few have survived. An example of this aspect of Margaret's work can be seen in a photograph of her mother at home, seated in front of a folding screen with paintings of native flora, which her daughter exhibited at the New Zealand and South Seas Exhibition at Dunedin in 1889-90.[3]

This country inherited from Victorian Britain a long association linking women with nature, expecially flowers, and this found expression not only in the fine and decorative arts but also in popular culture.[4] Women were photographed with bouquets in the garden and frequently painted with, and sometimes even as, flowers.[5] They were also named after plants; in colonial

New Zealand, Rata and Ngaio joined Ivy, Daisy and Rose as common names for girls. Flowers and femininity were closely allied in the home where women appliquéd cushions, crocheted doilies and embroidered traycloths with floral motifs. Many a carefully pressed flower was preserved as a souvenir in a scrapbook or birthday album.[6]

It is scarcely surprising that, as in Britain, flower painting came to be regarded as a suitable genre for female artists in colonial New Zealand. In 1883, an article entitled 'Flowers and Flower Painting', in the *Magazine of Art*, claimed that it seemed 'little short of heretical to destroy the association between Women and Flowers, when their resemblance in nature and aspect have been sung and celebrated for centuries'.[7] And in the following year, an essay in the same magazine, 'Women at Work: their Functions in Art', urged female readers to direct their special creativity to the domestic environment: 'to what is after all women's true mission – that of the presiding genius of the Home', where a feminine touch was not confined to the 'mere use of the Brush' but could 'give artistic beauty to a spray of ivy or feathery tamarisk by wreathing it round a mirror, and glorify a handful of red poppies by placing them in a sunny room in an antique jar'. [8]

Just how closely the arts of flower arranging and flower painting were allied is revealed in some letters from Margaret Stoddart to her friend and fellow painter, Rosa Dixon (1865-1960). In October 1895, when Margaret was chosen to organise floral displays for the opening of the Palette Club's spring exhibition, she based her theme on bush greens and clematis gathered on a social outing.[9] In April that year, she invited Rosa to enter the competition for table decorations at the annual chrysanthemum show to be held at the art gallery:

> I am really writing to tell you that the Chrysanthemum show is to be on May 3rd and 4th, and we expect you down here for it, don't expect much of the Chrysanthemums this year, but the pictures will most likely be on view as well. If I can get any flowers off my plants, what do you say to entering for table decorations, it would be rather fun, and we might possibly carry off a prize.[10]

Two weeks later she reported to Rosa how her arrangement of native berries and chrysanthemums was a source of controversy when it turned out to be the sole entry and had failed to gain a first prize:

> I think my second award was due chiefly to being the only competitor, also the judges Mrs Carrick and Mrs Irving thought that being an autumn show, only gorgeous colours should be used. I had only white and yellow out then and with native berries and coloured leaves they looked very well. Everyone said I should have had first prize which was better than the other way around.[11]

The tact, sensitivity and modesty expected of middle-class women prepared them poorly for the business of selling paintings, and it is interesting to

Anna Stoddart seated before the folding screen painted by Margaret Stoddart and shown at the New Zealand and South Seas Exhibition, Dunedin, 1889-90. Each panel shows representations of New Zealand flora.
M. Stoddart Album, Canterbury Museum, Christchurch

see Margaret take a much less conciliatory attitude with a prominent member of the Art Society, Captain C. Garsia, about lowering her prices. Her refusal was a measure of the seriousness with which she was beginning to take her career as an artist in the mid-1890s: 'The Art Exhibition is very badly attended now, and only a few more pictures are sold. Miss Clagston [sic] has sold three, but then her prices are very low. I hear Captain Garsia has been rating me for having them too high, but it's no use giving things away.'[12] At the 1895 exhibition Margaret's flower paintings had an average price of just over 6 guineas, double that of Miss Clagstoun's landscapes, and that of Frances Hodgkins's entry that year, *A Study of Girl's Head*, priced at 3 guineas. Margaret's negotiation with dealers and clients over prices was part of establishing her growing reputation as an artist:

> At present I am in a blissful state of calm, having just despatched my pictures to the Palette Club. They are also fairly approved of by the other members which also is satisfactory. Since they were in Gibb's shop I have had another offer for one, but as it is exactly half the price asked, at present I don't entertain it. Another sense of peace is that at last the Garsias have selected a picture instead of the one they let me have back last year. They chose the brown chrysanthemums which I worked up a good deal since you last saw it…[13]

The narration of day-to-day events, interspersed with snippets of what Margaret called 'shoppy talk', provides some insight into the way painting fitted into the lives of middle-class women who were starting out as artists. Margaret shared with Rosa some of the frustrations presented by commissions:

> …[the chrysanthemums] look lovely in my garden just now. I am right in the midst of a painting of them, at present they look utterly impossible, and to add to the situation the paper proves to be mildewed and has broken out in spots. It's enough to make one despair. It is a commission too, and I was given a number of the finest specimens of flowers, each of which has to be introduced. They are great lopping things which refuse to be arranged anyhow.[14]

Margaret, like other flower painters, frequently found her models at home in the garden. A family photograph shows her seated beside the conservatory, and next to the boxes where the seedlings were raised, which provided the subjects for her painting.

At the end of the nineteenth century, the chrysanthemum attracted worldwide attention from gardeners and artists. The practice of growing chrysanthemums in pots on the verandah became quite a fashion with women around this time, and the flower's popularity in this country was remarked upon in 1895 in an English publication, *The Gardener's Magazine*.[15] In 1882, *Nairn and Son's Special Price List of Bedding and Flowering Plants* included seventy-one kinds of chrysanthemums and 149 varieties of roses;[16] in their

Margaret Stoddart.
M. Stoddart Album, Canterbury Museum, Christchurch

catalogue ten years later, these figures had risen to 219 for chrysanthemums and 278 roses.[17] At the gallery, one reviewer described chrysanthemums as the 'latest artistic scare', with both male and female artists to be found 'worshipping at the shrine of "The flower of all" '.[18] From 1883, when Margaret began exhibiting, until 1899 (when she started to send work back from England), only the rose outstripped the chrysanthemum as a subject in her painting. Although works were often shown more than once on the Christchurch, Auckland, Wellington and Dunedin circuit, the exhibition catalogues list thirty-six paintings of roses, followed by twelve of chrysanthemums. Spring themes formed another favourite, with nine paintings of violets, primroses and fruit-tree blossoms, followed by four of Christmas roses. Christmas lilies and orchids, along with sweet peas, peonies and pansies, the narcissus and anenome, made only an occasional appearance. Roses and chrysanthemums lent themselves to splendid arrangements, and their choice blooms made them favourite motifs for floral decorations at home and for painting. In 1897, Margaret's painting of Gloire de Dijon roses won admiration from one of the country's most successful nurserymen. In his speech to the Christchurch Rose Society, Robert Nairn directed his audience to Miss Stoddart's painting, which captured 'with the truest exactness to nature' the way pale-coloured tea roses deepen in tone during the autumn months.[19]

In the 1890s, professional growers promoted new varieties of plants at flower shows, and there is every reason to believe that gardening trends influenced flower painting. Margaret's career coincided with a growing enthusiasm for gardening among women. From the beginning of European settlement in New Zealand, gardens had played an important part in providing shaded pathways and gentle walks, and flower beds, planted with

An arrangement of chrysanthemums. A photograph from Mary Stoddart's album.
M. Stoddart Album, Canterbury Museum, Christchurch

The Messrs Nairn and Sons Exhibit at the Christchurch Chrysanthemum Show in 1895.

Weekly Press, 9 May 1895

favourite blooms, helped to familiarise emigrants with their new surroundings. Substantial efforts were made to establish different varieties of English plants, and the garden was sometimes seen as a symbol of civilisation in contrast to the unfamiliar bush or stretch of plain that lay beyond. The cultural significance attached to gardening was emphasised in 1870 in *The Gardener's Chronicle for New Zealand*:

> It is scarcely necessary to observe upon the material benefits that the people of England and her dependencies derive from the taste for gardening which is so widely diffused among them… But it has a peculiar virtue for people situated like ourselves. For colonists whose special aim and desire it ever is to produce another ENGLAND wherever they settle – the study of these the most beautiful and delicate of Nature's productions is replete more than anything else with the reminiscences of the land from which we sprung.[20]

To what extent Stoddart's paintings of *Cherry Blossom*, 1890 and *Primroses*, 1891 evoked nostalgic memories in the hearts of gallery-goers in the late nineteenth century is not known, but her paintings kept alive the seasonal significance of flowers at Home. *Christmas Roses*, 1893 draws on well-known associations in the depiction of its delicate white petals emerging through dead leaves in the mid-winter garden. Because flower painting reflects nature's cycle, it also participates in the still life's traditional theme of transience, and, in 1892, a painting with this subject was shown as a series with *Spring Primroses*, *Summer Roses,* and *Autumn Chrysanthemums.*

Christmas Roses belonged to Miss Pearl Eugenia Hutton, the daughter of David Con Hutton (1843-1910), the foundation principal of the Dunedin School of Art, and its fidelity to nature and attention to detail exemplified the qualities her father upheld in his teaching.[21] Critical responses to Margaret's painting in her own time dwelt on the faithfulness of her observations, the accuracy of her drawing, her impeccable technique and her colour harmonies. As early as 1885, the *Lyttelton Times* declared that 'It would be hard to imagine Miss Stoddart doing any bad flower painting… all her exhibits are exquisite and should serve as models for several of our lady artists'.[22] Margaret's flower paintings were valued, above all, for their truth to nature, and this characteristic quickly established her reputation as the colony's foremost artist in this genre. When *Primroses* was shown at the Annual Exhibition of the Auckland Society of Arts in 1892, it attracted praise:

> Miss Stoddart, of Christchurch, is, as usual, unapproachable in flower painting. Her 'Primroses' depicts a small jar filled with these flowers, while an old tree pot is partially covered with a spray of apple blossom. The work is done with Miss Stoddart's characteristic carefulness. The tone of the primroses is very natural, and the general scheme of colour well carried out. The flowers are delicately and carefully treated. It is a pity that Auckland students of art do not devote more time to this branch of art, in which in this colony Miss Stoddart stands unrivalled.[23]

Cherry Blossom, 1890

Watercolour over pencil

440 x 345mm

Private Collection

Christmas Roses, 1893
Watercolour
514 × 677mm
Collection of Hocken Library, University of Otago, Dunedin

When *Primroses* was exhibited one month later in Christchurch, the painting gained similar approval in the newspaper there. The *Press* reviewer commented that:

> Miss Stoddart once more makes good her claim as *facile princeps* in flower painting with Primroses (110). With that wonderfully clever perception of hue to make contrast of colour which characterises so many of Miss Stoddart's productions, she has introduced a bunch of apple blossoms in the background, the colour which throws up in strong relief the pale loveliness of the flower of spring. This idea of effect, it may be noted, is also well worked out by the colour of the jar in which the flowers are placed. Altogether Miss Stoddart is to be congratulated on having in this the most charming as it is the most artistic flower piece in the exhibition. [24]

But whatever critical and financial success Margaret gained as an artist was limited by the modest status that flower painting had in colonial New Zealand, and elsewhere. Pamela Gerrish Nunn has argued that, in Victorian Britain, '…the woman-flower alliance turned out to be equally useful for covertly containing women's ambitions and for pragmatically promoting them'.[25] The association between femininity and flowers worked both for and against Margaret's success:

> Flowers are nowadays the especial property of our lady artists, and certainly a few of them have learnt to arrange and group them very prettily, and paint them well and naturally to boot. Miss Stoddart was our first 'floral artist' almost, and still remains *facile princeps* of the little band, who continue to send in their panels, plaques, and what not.[26]

In the traditional art hierarchy, still lifes were ranked at the bottom of

the scale, and this status was often reflected by lower prices. In critical reviews, still lifes frequently came last, together with flower paintings and sometimes watercolours. Although Margaret painted occasionally in oils, worked in landscape and achieved some success for figure studies such as *Study from Life. A Beach Comber*, 1888, it was her watercolour paintings of flowers that won her critical acclaim, enhancing her reputation but imposing limits on her professional ambitions.[27]

Also contributing to the lowly status of still-life and flower painting was the privileged position of landscape as the 'New Zealand subject'. Paintings of New Zealand's scenic grandeur had an acknowledged role in promoting the colony, at home and at international exhibitions, where they were prominently displayed. And, just as floral subjects were associated with femininity, the representation of spectacular scenery was regarded as predominantly masculine territory. Just how closely an artistic theme was sometimes related to gender appears in a letter to the *Press* urging male artists in Canterbury to leave the seaside sites to the ladies and to do their artistic duty by painting further afield:

> If our local artists who were born within sight of the glorious snow-clad mountains are not to paint them, who in the name of all that's beautiful are to?… The magnificent scenery of the west coast should be the happy hunting ground of New Zealand artists for all time. Let the ladies paint Sumner and Cave Rock, men who have strong limbs and brave hearts should seek their inspiration where hard climbing and plain food are the order of the day… Till our local artists wake up to these facts they are not doing their duty.[28]

Of course some women did sketch the landscape at Otira but many expeditions into the hinterland by female painters were in pursuit of flowers, not scenery.

FLOWER HUNTING IN THE COLONIAL LANDSCAPE

During the nineteenth century, botanical exploration and developments in the natural sciences combined with colonialism to stimulate a widespread interest in indigenous plants, which created a demand for flower paintings of native flora. In 1881, Marianne North's visit to New Zealand introduced the colony to an influential example of a woman artist whose painting had

M.O. Stoddart, *Study from Life. A Beach Comber,* charcoal, 768 × 500mm, exhibited at the Annual Exhibition of the Otago Art Society, 1888.

School of Fine Arts, University of Canterbury, Christchurch

Hoheria lyalli *(Ribbonwood),* 1890

Watercolour and bodycolour over traces of pencil on buff paper

270 × 375mm

Canterbury Museum, Christchurch

Hebe salicifolia (Koromiko), 1896
Watercolour and bodycolour over traces of
pencil on grey buff paper
360 × 270mm
Canterbury Museum, Christchurch

Mr and Mrs E.H. Featon, *The Art Album of New Zealand Flora; being a systematic and popular description of the native flowering plants of New Zealand and their adjacent islands,* Wellington, 1889.

achieved recognition in London. Although her arrival went largely unrecorded in the press, it was nevertheless an important event in colonial circles. North was the most celebrated female traveller and flower painter of the Victorian period, and she was also a cousin of John Davies Enys, who was a close friend of Edward Chudleigh and an acquaintance of the Stoddarts. He is also known to have taken some interest in Margaret's painting.[29]

Enys shared his cousin's passion for botanising, and their correspondence reveals that she kept him informed about the progress of her gallery.[30] In 1882, the Marianne North Gallery, built at the artist's own expense, opened at Royal Kew Gardens, London and displayed an extensive collection of paintings of native plants, which she had completed on her travels and presented to the nation.[31] North's colourful depiction of the plants and flowers of five continents painted within their natural habitats was reported widely in the press. The *Magazine of Art* emphasised the scientific importance of North's undertaking and the popularity of her theme:

> The result is a collection which is every whit as generally interesting as it is scientifically instructive and valuable. We have Sir Joseph Hooker's word that it is not possible to overrate its scientific importance and usefulness in connection with the gardens, plant-houses, and museums at Kew; and it is more than likely that future generations will have a better opportunity of appreciating the gift than is afforded at the present time, since many of the scenes depicted are slowly but surely disapppearing before the ploughs and herds, the fires and the axes, of the colonist and the pioneer. The forests and the wild flowers fade away for ever before the march of civilisation; and it is only by such pictures as Miss North's that the majesty and wonder of the one, and the gorgeousness and delicacy of the other, can be recorded or adequately suggested… Its chief interest is essentially scientific; and, since there are few things in creation which appeal more pleasantly and constantly to the human mind than flowers, it is also essentially popular.[32]

The *Illustrated London News* described it as 'incomparably the most complete, and at the same time the most accurate series of illustrations of the flora of the world in existence', enabling the viewer at Kew to proceed 'as it were upon a botanical expedition all round the world'.[33]

North's visit coincided with a period when women artists here were painting the native flora and by the end of the decade a succession of illustrated books by resident New Zealand artists had appeared: Mr and Mrs Featon's *The Art Album of New Zealand Flora; being a systematic and popular description of the native flowering plants of New Zealand and their adjacent islands* (1887-89), Mrs Charles Hetley's (Georgina B. Hetley), *The Native Flowers of New Zealand. Illustrated in colours in the best style of modern chromo-litho art, from drawings coloured to nature* (1887-1888) and Emily Harris's three books, *New Zealand Flowers, New Zealand Berries* and *New Zealand Ferns* (1890).[34]

Paintings of New Zealand flowers featured regularly at annual art society shows, as well as at the numerous intercolonial exhibitions held at home and overseas. In 1886-87, four paintings of native flora by Margaret Stoddart were '…among the large display of this class of work exhibited by colonial ladies' at the Colonial and Indian Exhibition in London, where she gained a favourable mention in a review of New Zealand art in the *Magazine of Art*: 'The majority of the flower pieces aim less at decorative effect than scientific accuracy. Miss Margaret Stoddart's "In the Bush" and "Mountain Daisies" may be noted as successful treatment of still-life from an artistic point of view. The latter painting is not merely a good botanical study but an agreeable essay in decoration.'[35]

Between 1883 and 1899, Margaret showed no fewer than thirty-five paintings of native flora at art society exhibitions, including depictions of

The Marianne North Gallery, Royal Botanic Gardens, Kew, England.

Celmisia coriacea *(Mountain Daisy)*, 1897
Watercolour and bodycolour over traces of
pencil on grey buff paper
355 × 270mm
Canterbury Museum, Christchurch

Marianne North, *View of the Otira Gorge*,
oil on paper, 510 × 353mm.
Marianne North Gallery, Royal Botanic Gardens, Kew, England

Mountain Lily *(Ranunculus lyalli),* (c. 1885)
Watercolour over traces of pencil
480 × 360mm
Collection of the Troup Family

the Mountain Lily, now known as Mount Cook Lily, Ribbonwood, Mountain Daisy and the Native Clematis, which was by far the most popular flower with colonial painters. Clematis, known as the 'harbinger of spring', was by this time a favourite garden plant enjoyed for 'its pure white flowers, often produced in immense abundance'.[36] In *The Art Album of New Zealand Flora,* the Featons refer to it as virgin's bower, and to the purity and chastity of its white flowers.[37]

Margaret's representation of native flora in the 1880s and 1890s can be divided broadly into two groups. Plants were painted either against a plain background, seen in *Titoki Berries,* 1886, which followed a format frequently used in botanical illustration, or pictured as if growing in their natural habitats. Margaret completed numerous studies of plants painted in water-colours and opaque bodycolour on a green, or grey-buff paper, and although these were valued for their botanical accuracy, they also appealed to a popular audience who appreciated her artistic interpretation. A comparison between *Titoki Berries*, 1886 and *Celmisia coriacea (Mountain Daisy)*, 1897 reveals her development towards a freer handling and increasingly painterly technique.

Alpine Flowers from North Otago (Herpolirion novae zealandiae), 1886 was exhibited in 1886 at the Annual Exhibition of the Otago Art Society in Dunedin, and in the same year at Christchurch. Its composition and attention to detail related to Victorian painting and to the ideas of John Ruskin, the period's most influential art critic, who directed students to meticulous recording of nature in detailed representations. The practice of painting plants growing in their natural habitats, seen in *Mountain Lily,* (c. 1885), was employed by many artists around this time. According to Sir Joseph Hooker, the director at Kew, Marianne North's way of depicting 'plants in their homes' bestowed 'a living interest to the scenes and a high scientific one too'.[38] This also resulted in landscapes of the floral or botanical environment, such as North's *View of the Otira Gorge* with its detailed depiction of the distinctive vegetation in this region. The connection between plants and places is characteristic of many of Margaret's landscape paintings, including *On the Beach, Cheviot*, 1896, as well as later paintings such as *Sand Dunes,* (c. 1920) and *Yellow Lupins,* (c. 1925). Her representation of alpine flora in the foreground of *Stocking Glacier from Hooker Valley,* (c. 1932), shown at the Annual Exhibition of the Canterbury Society of Arts in 1932, has clear links with these early concerns.

Although their importance has been largely overlooked, flower painters played a significant part in the colonial period by familiarising settlers with the local flora, as well as by drawing attention to how colonisation was putting the native environment at risk. In *The Art Album of New Zealand Flora*, produced in this country and lavishly illustrated with coloured lithographs for the colonial market, the Featons expressed their desire to show the public the singularity and diversity of New Zealand plant species in the 'hope that their labours may tend to make many friends to help conserve our beautiful native flora…'.[39] Georgina Hetley strongly condemned the wanton burning of the bush that she encountered all too often on her journeys: 'The beautiful forest with its flowers and ferns is fast disappearing before the tide of cultivation…'[40]

Flower-hunting expeditions allowed women to escape from the constraints that often governed their daily lives. Marianne North, whose journeys encompassed five continents, was the period's archetypal female traveller and, in New Zealand, Georgina Hetley left an account of her trips around the North and South Islands by steamship, rail and coach. She subsequently went on to Royal Kew Gardens to complete the research for

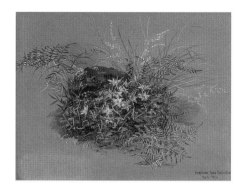

Alpine Flowers from North Otago (Herpolirion novae zealandiae), 1886
Watercolour and bodycolour on dull green paper
270 × 355mm
Canterbury Museum, Christchurch

On the Beach, Cheviot, 1896
Watercolour and bodycolour
392 × 565mm
Collection of Dunedin Public Art Gallery

Sand Dunes, (c. 1920)
Watercolour and bodycolour over charcoal
245 x 345mm
Collection of Rangi Ruru Girls' School, Christchurch

her book. On a more modest scale, painting excursions also enlivened the daily routines of Emily Harris's hard existence in Nelson. A group of photographs and sketches from Margaret Stoddart's album record the journey she made in April 1896 along the West Coast Road to paint the alpine flowers, and they graphically illustrate the freedom that an expedition provided.

The idea of such a trip had surfaced the previous spring when she confided, in a letter to Rosa Dixon, an impulse to forsake her Fendalton garden:

> How does your garden look now? Nearly all the bulbs here are over, my primroses are still bright, and the roses are almost showing colour. It makes it seem late in the year doesn't it? I had a beautiful plan of going off to the West Coast road when the mountain lilies were out, if only this exhibition were successful it's almost time for it. The [illegible] of spring is one gets so full of brilliant ideas it's quite a pain not to be able to carry them all out…[41]

The party that started out in the following autumn consisted of Margaret and Rosa, and at least two other people, whose identity is uncertain. One was a man, possibly Margaret's brother, Jack, or Rosa's brother, Marmaduke, and the other, who acted as the photographer, was probably Margaret's sister, Mary, who shared her enthusiasm for the outdoors and whose album at the Canterbury Museum contains a collection of pictures revealing her strong interest in photography.[42] Margaret completed several paintings of alpine plants and

Yellow Lupins, (c. 1925)
Watercolour and bodycolour over charcoal
450 x 480mm
Collection of Manawatu Art Gallery, Palmerston North

flowers collected on this trip, including a study of an alpine gentian that she later presented to the Canterbury Museum. The six-day excursion occupies three pages in the album and begins with vignettes of the journey arranged around a watercolour of the alpine gentian. Photographs and sketches of the

Stocking Glacier from Hooker Valley, (c. 1932)
Watercolour and bodycolour over charcoal
478 × 438mm
Collection of the Museum of New Zealand Te Papa
Tongarewa. Negative no. B037393.

53

Above: On the West Coast Road, April 1896 (detail).

Right: M.O. Stoddart, the *Ranunculus lyalli* (Mount Cook Lily) (left page) and the attempted ascent of Mount Cook in November 1893 (right page) with centre photograph by G.E. Mannering, Tom Fyfe (left) and Marmaduke Dixon at the Haast Ridge bivouac; photograph on right by Tom Fyfe, the first use of skis on Mount Cook, Marmaduke Dixon (left) and G.E. Mannering on the Grand Plateau, November 1893.

Below: On the West Coast Road, April 1896.

landscape, vegetation and of the group's activities are interspersed on each page to provide a record of the expedition. The photographs of Margaret and Rosa boiling the billy and enjoying a picnic outdoors were taken with a hand-held quarter-plate camera; they convey some idea of what the experience meant to these women in colonial society.

Margaret's album also includes some photographs by G.E. Mannering and Tom Fyfe of an attempted ascent of Mount Cook which they made with Marmaduke Dixon in November 1893.[43] Marmaduke took an active part in climbing and exploring the Mount Cook region. In 1891, he was one of the three founders of the New Zealand Alpine Club. He was also a close companion of Margaret around this time. To mark their expedition, on the accompanying page Margaret carefully mounted a photograph of the *Ranunculus lyalli, or Mount Cook Lily,* which she combined with her painting in a kind of collage.

THE CHATHAM ISLANDS

The album also contains photographs of trips further afield, to Australia and to the Chatham Islands, which lie about 800 kilometres east of the South Island of New Zealand. Margaret first visited the Chathams in 1886-87 and she returned to the islands in 1891, with a party accompanying Bishop Julius for the consecration of St Augustine's at Te One, 8 kilometres from Waitangi on Chatham, the largest island in the group. Known by its original inhabitants, the Moriori, as Rekohu, 'Misty Skies', and then by Maori as Wharekauri, the island had been given its European name 100 years earlier when Lieutenant William Broughton sailed around its northern coast in the brig *Chatham.*[44] Margaret spent most of her time at Wharekauri on the northern coast of Chatham, where she stayed with a family friend, Mabel

Potts of Governors Bay, who had come there in 1881 with her husband, Edward Chudleigh, who had established a sheep-run in 1866. She made several trips around the island and she was also a frequent visitor at the Shands' homestead at Te Whakaru, where Archibald Watson Shand and his wife Elizabeth had settled with their family in the 1860s.

Margaret's arrival, on 19 April 1886, coincided with the onset of one of the bleakest and wettest winters Edward Chudleigh had experienced. His diary gives some idea of the harsh and isolated environment. He noted on 28 August: 'Snow fell last night & snow & hail fell in showers all day… as to real sun there has been none for months'; on 31 August: 'I hope the new month will commence new weather for the last four have been enough to make one tired of life'.[45]

Margaret's long stay at the Chathams, until 7 June 1887, allowed her to paint its distinctive flora at different times of the year. She included endemic plants such as *Corokia macrocarpa (Chatham Islands Korokio)*, 1886, *Pseudopanax chathamicum (Chatham Islands Lancewood)*, 1886 and *Myrsine chathamica (Chatham Islands Matipo)*, 1886, which were all painted with their coloured berries in winter. In the summer months, she painted some flowering plants, including the golden blossoms of the *Senecio huntii (Rautini)*, 1886, the delicate *Veronica chathamica*, 1887, which grows on the island's rocky coastlines, the *Calystegia soldanella (Sand Convolvulus)*, 1887, the *Geranium traversii (Chatham Cranesbill)*, 1886, and the low trailing bushes of the *Pimelea arenaria (Sand Daphne)*, 1886, known for its delicate white flowers that spread out above the shoreline.[46]

Margaret Stoddart's collection of paintings at the Canterbury Museum includes at least fifteen studies of Chatham Islands flora, although it is impossible to know whether these were among the 'drawings of plants' that the artist presented to the museum on 17 March 1907, or if they were acquired earlier. In 1889, the Museum Committee discussed the possibility of a commission for paintings to be placed with the dried plant specimens in the herbarium and, in the following year, they purchased twelve studies of native flora.[47]

Above: On the West Coast Road, April 1896.
M.O. Stoddart Album, Canterbury Museum, Christchurch

Above left: Wharekauri, Chatham Islands.
Weekly Press, 1 September 1897

Below: Te Whakaru, Chatham Islands. Photograph by Alfred Martin, 1877, and watercolour by M.O. Stoddart, 1886.
M.O. Stoddart Album, Canterbury Museum, Christchurch

Near right: **Pseudopanax chathamicum** *(Chatham Islands Lancewood),* 1886
Watercolour and bodycolour over traces of pencil on buff paper
360 × 270mm
Canterbury Museum, Christchurch

Far right: **Myrsine chathamica** *(Chatham Islands Matipo),* 1886
Watercolour and bodycolour over traces of pencil on buff paper
360 × 270mm
Canterbury Museum, Christchurch

Near right: **Corokia macrocarpa** *(Chatham Islands Korokio),* 1886
Watercolour and bodycolour over traces of underdrawing on dull green paper
360 × 270mm
Canterbury Museum, Christchurch

Far right: **Senecio huntii** *(Rautini),* 1886
Watercolour and bodycolour over traces of pencil on buff paper
355 × 270mm
Canterbury Museum, Christchurch

Veronica chathamica, now known as *Hebe chathamica,* **and Calystegia soldanella,** *(Sand Convolvulus),* 1887
Watercolour and bodycolour over traces of pencil on dull green paper
270 × 375mm
Canterbury Museum, Christchurch

Pimelea arenaria (Sand Daphne) **and Geranium**
traversii (Chatham cranesbill), 1886
Watercolour and bodycolour over traces of pencil on buff
paper
270 × 375mm
Canterbury Museum, Christchurch

Julius von Haast, the museum's director, believed that science and art
should go hand in hand, and he would have agreed with Ruskin's idea that
art should be the interpreter of nature. He was also aware of the value of
paintings in reaching a wider public, and he had commissioned John Gully
for landscapes on two occasions.[48] On 28 November 1887, about five months
after Margaret returned from the Chathams, the Museum Committee, which
at this time included Thomas Potts, purchased 'two pictures of Chatham
Island scenery from Miss Stoddart at a cost of £5.0.0.'.[49] One of these, *Moriori*

Moriori Tree Carving, Chatham Islands, also known as
Carved Trees, Chatham Islands (Dendroglyphs), 1887
Sepia monochrome
225 × 290mm
Canterbury Museum, Christchurch

Map of the Chatham Islands showing Wharekauri, where Margaret stayed with the Chudleighs, and Te Whakaru, where she visited the Shands.

Above right: **Cape Young, Chatham Islands,** painted on 14 February 1889 by Margaret Stoddart under her own birth-date on 3 October, in Nina Jones's Birthday Album. Bett Collection, Nelson Provincial Museum

M.O. Stoddart, *The prisoners' huts on Orea Flat, overlooking Waitangi Bay*, 1886 (above) with the Lament of Te Kooti, translated by H. Parata at Otaki, January 1893 (below). M.O. Stoddart Album, Canterbury Museum, Christchurch

Tree Carving, Chatham Islands, 1887, was exhibited at the Second Winter Exhibition of the Canterbury Society of Arts. It depicted the carvings of stylised human figures made by the Moriori in the kopi or karaka groves which, according to Potts, were to be found close to the Wharekauri run.[50] A second painting, *Moriori Burial Place, Chatham Islands*, 1887 (Canterbury Museum), depicting the skeletal remains of Moriori uncovered in the sand on a windswept coastal landscape, was shown at the same exhibition. The Moriori custom of burying their dead in the sand facing the sea meant that their bones were frequently uncovered by the elements. The burial grounds along the beaches were of ethnographical interest in the Victorian period and skeletal remains, along with Moriori artifacts, were collected freely and with curiosity by some European visitors and settlers on the Chathams.[51]

Alexander Shand played a major role in attempting to record Moriori traditions, customs and language. His research, published between 1892 and 1898 by the Polynesian Society, reflected contemporary interest in the islands' indigenous people.[52] In 1883, the Moriori population had dropped to thirty-two from 1600 in 1835, and they were viewed in colonial society as a dying race. Margaret's painting, *Near Wharekauri Beach, Chatham Islands, Moriori Skull*, 1886-87 (Hocken Library, University of Otago), of a skull, a traditional still-life symbol, with bones, a paua shell and a whale tooth in a bold close-up composition on an expanse of beach, reflects these perceptions.

Either on horseback or on foot, Margaret visited the principal historic sites on Chatham Island and, in the summer, she caught the steamer from Whangaroa to Pitt Island, known for its rocky coastline and striking scenery. She became familiar with the island's landscape and developed an interest in its troubled past. In 1889, she painted a picture of Cape Young under her own birth-date, 3 October, in the birthday book belonging to Nina Jones, a friend and flower painter who lived at Nelson. The cliffs at Cape Young, named by Broughton in 1791, are at the eastern end of the northern coast of Chatham and a few hours' walk from Wharekauri. In 1886, Margaret made a drawing of the Hau Hau prisoners' huts overlooking Waitangi Bay, where Te Kooti had been wrongfully imprisoned until he escaped in 1868. Several years later, on the same page, she pasted a sheet of paper with some verses from the *Lament of Te Kooti,* translated at Otaki in January 1893 by H. Parata.[53] Margaret visited Rangiatea in 1893, and she framed Te Kooti's lament with a painted border copied from the hammerhead shark design that is found on the kowhaiwhai in the great Maori church at Otaki.

Portrait of Ellis Rowan from her newspaper cutting book.
Manuscript 2203, National Library of Australia, Canberra

An exhibition of flower painting in Melbourne

It was early in 1894 that Margaret's meeting with Ellis Rowan, Australia's leading flower painter, took place. Rowan came to New Zealand in late 1893, and she embarked on an extensive tour through both islands, which included an expedition to Otira. She stayed at Coker's Hotel in Christchurch from 12 to 20 March and, from 3 to 7 April, saw Margaret's paintings at the Art Gallery and subsequently paid her a visit. In 1894, the *Press* reproduced an excerpt from the Australian *Town and Country Journal,* in which 'Mrs Rowan, speaking of Miss Stoddart's collection of pictures and sketches, said: – 'It was a new revelation to me to see such work hidden away, and I think she stands without a rival the first and foremost of our flower painters… Her grouping, colouring, form and harmony were perfect.'[54] Rowan recalled these events four years later in an account of her travels, *A Flower-Hunter in Queensland and New Zealand,* remembering also how 'Even here [Christchurch] everyone was shivering, but I forgot the weather amongst Miss Stodart's [*sic*] beautiful flower paintings in the Art Gallery. I had the pleasure of meeting her, and next morning went to see her whole collection.'[55]

Ellis Rowan enjoyed considerable fame on account of her success at the 1888 Centennial Exhibition in Melbourne, where her painting, *Chrysanthemums,* had gained a first order of merit, above artists such as Frederick McCubbin (1855-1917), Tom Roberts (1856-1931) and Arthur Streeton (1867-1943). She also won numerous awards for flower paintings in the New Zealand, Victorian and Queensland display courts.[56] In the following year she added to her reputation at the New Zealand and South Seas Exhibition in Dunedin, 1889-90 and, in 1890, when the National Gallery of Victoria purchased two flower paintings.

Rowan was an important contact for Margaret Stoddart. She was seventeen years older than Margaret, with a charming and compelling personality, and a feminine and youthful appearance that belied her determination to succeed.[57] Their shared enthusiasm for flower painting and similarities in their background laid the basis for their acquaintance. Rowan's grandfather was a naturalist, and she had the benefit of social advantages that encouraged her early involvement in painting and natural history.[58] She was the daughter of a successful Victorian pastoralist and stock and station agent and, after her marriage in 1873 to Charles Frederic Rowan, an English army officer serving in New Zealand, the couple lived briefly in New Plymouth before returning to Australia, where they settled in Melbourne. Rowan gained her first medal at the Intercolonial Exhibition in Melbourne in 1872, and she continued to paint and exhibit after her marriage, and after her husband's death in 1892. Some years later, she was to claim, in dramatic fashion, that it was after her meeting with Marianne North, who visited Australia in 1880, that she became her 'devoted admirer' and found her true direction.[59]

Rowan's claim prompts some reflection on the affinities and alliances between female artists who worked in this genre in the Victorian and colonial world, and which are borne out by Margaret's arrival in 1894 in Melbourne. On 21 August, the *Argus* reported: 'Mrs Ellis Rowan has been the means of bringing into notice a young lady from Christchurch, in New Zealand, who is at present staying in Melbourne, whose skill as a flower painter resembles her own, yet with such differences as result from individual temperament and touch'. The article drew particular attention to Margaret's accuracy of drawing and sense of colour, and closed with a favourable description of her work:

> Among the most beautiful of the drawings she has brought with her are groups of chrysanthemums, of Gloire de Dijon roses, violets and maidenhair fern, fruit blossoms, cactus, camellias, and the catkins of some of the indigenous trees and shrubs of New Zealand. To these must be added a number of studies of the flora of that colony, and also of Chatham Island, which appears to be singularly rich in wild flowers and native berries. The trustees of the National Gallery in Sydney have purchased one of Miss Stoddart's flower pieces, and they have only to be seen in order to be appreciated by all lovers of the beautiful branch of art to which she has devoted herself, although it is only right to add that she appears qualified to shine as a landscape painter also.[60]

A report in the *Sun* drew attention to a painted plate that had won 'the especial commendation of Mrs Ellis Rowan herself', and to an 'out-of-doors study, painted in the Melbourne Botanical Gardens, of an open-hearted white camellia'.[61] These advance notices preceded an exhibition of Margaret's flower painting held in October at the studio of James Peele, Old Court, on Swanston Street, which also attracted favourable reviews in the Melbourne papers.[62]

Margaret's success was reported with some satisfaction in New Zealand:

> We do not quote the above remarks because we think Miss Stoddart's artistic work is not appreciated here and because we need to be told how excellent it is; but it

is pleasant to find the opinion of local art lovers and critics endorsed by such a paper as the *Argus*, and doubly pleasant to find one of our young artists striking out into a wider world and more than holding her own in it.[63]

She was one of several New Zealand women who gained some recognition in Australia in the 1890s. Grace Joel first left Dunedin in 1888-89 for the National Gallery School in Melbourne[64] and returned there in 1891-94, winning the 1893 Ramsay Prize for a painting from the nude.[65] Dora Meeson arrived from Christchurch in 1895, also to study at the National Gallery School, and later that year she gained the prize for a poster of Minerva in a Sydney competition. In the following year she competed for the National Gallery Travelling Scholarship.[66] Margaret reported on Dora's progress in a letter to Rosa:

Isn't Dora Meeson's success splendid I had a letter from her just before she heard the result of her picture, she thought very little of her work which she declared 'vulgar' in style, though it would be hard to prevent that in such a subject. Still as it was judged by the Trustees of the National Gallery in Sydney, and all the best students were competing, the honour to her was all the greater. She is coming home for Xmas, but only for the holidays, I believe she has a very good chance for a travelling scholarship, which means going Home of course and a Continental Course… I had a letter last week from a Melbourne girl who takes the other view of Dora's success. It seems to have caused great bitterness among the Melbourne girls at the gallery, over whose heads she was advanced, and who of course declare that New Zealand girls are nothing but 'bounce and conceit'. As they all seem to have been pretty successful over there, perhaps that is how they earn such bad opinion.[67]

This letter reveals that Margaret was corresponding with a network of women artists and keeping herself informed about their progress. So far she had developed her own career with a mixture of enterprise and discretion, and she had won approval in colonial society. But to compete professionally she needed to travel to Europe, and to broaden her horizons. Margaret's letter highlights how taking on the identity of a professional artist meant significant changes in the lives of this generation of women. In 1895, Margaret Stoddart and Rosa Dixon reached their thirtieth year, and they were both unmarried. The decision to become a professional painter meant taking on the challenge of leaving New Zealand for a more independent way of life.

In 1895, Margaret was living at Lismore Lodge in Fendalton, Christchurch, with her mother and sisters, but a couple of years later they returned once more to Diamond Harbour. This time they moved into the 'big house', the grand two-storeyed residence, built by Harvey Hawkins, which became known in 1913 as Godley House. Hawkins had been granted an extension of his mortgage, which meant the capital did not have to be repaid until 1893, but on 5 September 1894 he was declared bankrupt and all the land that had

The Stoddarts' home, known as Godley House, where Margaret lived with her mother and sisters at Diamond Harbour.
M. Stoddart Album, Canterbury Museum, Christchurch

The Misses Bradley on a visit to the Stoddarts at Diamond Harbour.
M. Stoddart Album, Canterbury Museum, Christchurch

View of Lyttelton Harbour.
M. Stoddart Album, Canterbury Museum, Christchurch

Margaret and her sisters at Lyttelton Harbour.
M. Stoddart Album, Canterbury Museum, Christchurch

been sold to him in 1876 was transferred back to the trustees.[68] It was probably in 1897 that Mrs Stoddart and her daughters first took up residence at the house, although they may have stayed there even earlier. It was an imposing home with a wide verandah ornamented with cast-iron lace, and with marble fireplaces in the downstairs reception rooms. Chudleigh visited them there on 23 March 1897: 'Went to Diamond Harbour and remained the night. Mrs Stoddart, Marjorie [Chudleigh's name for Margaret], Mary and Agnes at home. It is a very nice place but cut off very much.'[69] Some photographs in Mary's album provide an idea of their life together at Diamond Harbour and the long walks that the sisters made around the bays where they had spent their childhood.

In 1897, Frances took up a position as the headmistress at Toi Toi Valley School, Nelson. Margaret seems to have stayed on at Diamond Harbour probably until early in 1898. Her friend Rosa remained in New Zealand until 1901, when she sailed for Europe on the RMS *Arcadia*; also on board was Frances Hodgkins. A letter from Frances to Rosa, written on 1 October in the previous year, shows that by 1900 Rosa had made up her mind to leave as well:

Just a few lines to tell you I am so glad you have decided or nearly decided to go Home. A state of indecision is very unsettling is it not? You will feel much happier now you have finally made up your mind… Is Miss Stoddart still at Home? or is she coming out this year. Dora Meeson is going to settle somewhere in England and take a studio – there is no talk of her coming out to N.Z. again…[70]

NOTES:

1. *Lyttelton Times*, 27 December 1882, p.5.

2. *Lyttelton Times*, 8 March 1883 p.6.

3. New Zealand and South Seas Exhibition, Dunedin, 1889-1890, Colonial Oil Paintings: 116 Folding Screen (upon each panel are displayed representations of New Zealand flora).

4. Pamela Gerrish Nunn, *Problem Pictures: Women and Men in Victorian Painting*, London, 1995, pp.29-47; in New Zealand, flower painting and its links with women's culture are examined perceptively by Ann Elias, 'New Zealand Still Life and Flower Painting 1880-1940', Unpublished PhD thesis, University of Auckland, 1991.

5. For example, Grace Joel, *A Rose 'Midst Poppies* (Robert McDougall Art Gallery). Joel's well-known symbolical image of a woman surrounded by poppies was exhibited at the Annual Exhibition of the Otago Art Society, 1896, as 32, *A Rose 'Midst Poppies*, and is linked to a flourishing tradition of similar works in Victorian painting in this period.

6. Jennifer Isaacs, *The Gentle Arts: 200 Years of Australian Domestic and Decorative Arts*, Sydney, 1987.

7. Katherine de Mattos, 'Flowers and Flower-Painters', *Magazine of Art*, 1883, p.453, quoted by Nunn, p.30.

8. Leader Scott, 'Women at Work: their functions in art', *Magazine of Art*, 1884, p.99.

9. Letter to Rosa Dixon from Margaret Stoddart, Fendalton, 2 October 1895.

10. Letter to Rosa Dixon from Margaret Stoddart, Fendalton, 20 April [1895].

11. Letter to Rosa Dixon from Margaret Stoddart, Fendalton, 14 May [1895]. Margaret's failure to gain a first prize was commented on in the *Weekly Press*, 9 May 1895, p.40.

12. Letter to Rosa Dixon from Margaret Stoddart, Fendalton, 20 April [1895].

13. Letter to Rosa Dixon from Margaret Stoddart, Fendalton, 2 October 1895.

14. Letter to Rosa Dixon from Margaret Stoddart, Fendalton, 14 May [1895].

Looking at the view at Lyttelton Harbour.

M. Stoddart Album, Canterbury Museum, Christchurch

15. Thelma Strongman, *The Gardens of Canterbury*, Wellington, 1984, p.41.

16. Katherine Raine and John P. Adam, '1860s-1900 Victorian Gardens', in *A History of the Garden in New Zealand*, ed. Malcolm Bradbury, Auckland, 1995, p.103.

17. *Nairn and Sons General Descriptive Catalogue 1892-93*, Ephemera Collection, Alexander Turnbull Library, National Library, Wellington.

18. *Triad*, 15 May, 1894, p.9.

19. 'A Paper read by Mr Robert Nairn at the Annual Meeting of the Canterbury Rose Society', *Press*, 24 March 1897, p.3.

20. Felix Wakefield, *The Gardener's Chronicle for New Zealand*, pp.4-5, quoted by Katherine Raine and John P. Adam, '1860s-1900 Victorian Gardens', in *A History of the Garden in New Zealand*, ed. Malcolm Bradbury, pp.102-103.

21. I am indebted to Rosemary Entwisle at the Hocken Library, University of Otago, Dunedin, for information about the Huttons.

22. *Lyttelton Times*, 12 March 1885, p.5.

23. *New Zealand Herald*, 4 March 1892, p.6.

24. *Press*, 12 April 1892, p.6.

25. Nunn, p.30.

26. *Lyttelton Times*, 17 November 1890, p.5.

27. 'Miss Stoddart's carefully drawn and picturesque "Old Beachcomber", which took the Otago Art Society's Medal, is wonderful for a lady who has made her reputation in flower drawing and who is but a first year student in the life class.' *Lyttelton Times*, 8 February 1889, p.3.

28. *Press*, 21 July 1893, p.3.

29. 'Rain all day. J.D. Enys and I called on Mrs Stoddart and saw Margery's [*sic*] pictures. Mrs Stoddart is a clever woman and her girls are fine and clever as well.' E.C. Richards, 20 June 1887, *Diary of E.R. Chudleigh 1862-1921*, Macmillan Brown Library, University of Canterbury.

30. John Davies Enys (1837-1912) Papers MS Papers 670, National Library, Wellington.

31. The Marianne North Gallery was completed in 1885 and contained 848 paintings. Laura Ponsonby, *Marianne North at Kew Gardens,* Exeter, 1990, p.124.

32. H.V. Barnett, 'Miss Marianne North's Paintings at Kew', *Magazine of Art*, 1882, p.431.

33. *Illustrated London News*, 17 June 1882, p.587, 24 June 1882, p.616.

34. F. Bruce Sampson, *Early New Zealand Botanical Art*, Auckland, 1985, p.102.

35. J.A. Blaikie, 'Art in New Zealand', *Magazine of Art*, 1887, p.36.

36. Mrs Charles Hetley, *The Native Flowers of New Zealand*, London, 1888, p.3.

37. Mr and Mrs E.H. Featon, *The Art Album of New Zealand Flora*, Wellington, 1889, p.2.

38. Letter to Marianne North from Sir Joseph Hooker, 3 April 1888, in Brenda E. Moon, 'Marianne North's Recollections of a Happy Life: how they came to be written and published', *Journal of the Society for the Bibliography of Natural History*, Vol. 8 (4), pp.497-505.

39. Mr and Mrs E.H. Featon, p.x.

40. Mrs Charles Hetley, p.3.

41. Letter to Rosa Dixon from Margaret Stoddart, Fendalton, Christchurch, 2 October 1895, Private Collection.

42. M. Stoddart Album, Canterbury Museum, Christchurch; Margaret's older sister, Frances, was a member of the Nelson Camera Club. See Rosalina McCarthy, 'Women and the Nelson Camera Club 1888-1900, *New Zealand Journal of Photography,* 17 November 1994, p.16.

43. Jim Wilson, *The Story of Mount Cook*, Christchurch, 1968, pp.77-87.

44. Te Miria Kate Wills-Johnson, 'Introduction', *The Chatham Islands: Heritage and Conservation*, Christchurch, 1996.

45. 28 August & 31 August 1886. E.C. Richards, *Diary of E.R. Chudleigh, 1862-1921.*

46. L. Cockayne, *New Zealand Plants and their Story*, Wellington, 1967, p.28; and David Given, 'Flora', *The Chatham Islands Heritage and Conservation*, Christchurch, 1996, pp.80-92.

47. Canterbury Museum Accession Register 1891-1933, 18 March 1907; Canterbury College Thirty-Fifth Annual Report 1908, p.31; Canterbury Museum Committee Minutes, 23 December 1889 & 17 March 1890. Records, University of Canterbury, Christchurch.

48. Von Haast's association with artists is emphasised by Leonard Bell, 'Nicholas Chevalier's Journey Through Canterbury in 1866: Contexts and Connections', *Bulletin of New Zealand Art History*, Vol. 14, 1993, p.102; Von Haast died on 16 August 1887.

49. Canterbury Museum Committee Minutes, 28 November 1887. Records, University of Canterbury, Christchurch.

50. The function and meaning of these carvings is no longer known but they are thought to represent individuals possibly in commemoration of kinsfolk and ancestors. Michael King, *Moriori: A People Rediscovered*, Auckland, 1989, p.36; T.H. Potts, 'Meeting with a Moriori', in *Out in the Open*, Christchurch, 1882.

51. Michael King, pp.101-102.

52. Alexander Shand, *The Moriori People of the Chatham Islands: their history and traditions*, Wellington, 1911. p.v; the Te Iwi Moriori Trust Board was consulted and did not consent to the inclusion of illustrations of *Moriori Burial Place, Chatham Islands*, 1887 and *Near Wharekauri Beach, Chatham Islands, Moriori Skull*, 1886-87.

53. 'The song is Waiata 14 in Hamiora Aparoa's collection, "E pa to hau he wini raro", dated about 1871. It is an adaptation of an earlier lament from Ngati Apakura hapu of Waikato.' Judith Binney, *Redemption Songs: A Life of Te Kooti Arikirangi Te Turuki*, Auckland, 1995, p.563.

54. *Press*, 3 September 1894, p.4; I would like to acknowledge my indebtedness to Judith McKay for supplying the exact dates of Ellis Rowan's stay in Christchurch.

55. Ellis Rowan, *A Flower-Hunter in Queensland and New Zealand,* Sydney, 1898, p.251.

56. Caroline Clemente, *Australian Watercolours 1802-1926 in the Collection of the National Gallery of Victoria*, Melbourne, 1991, p.68.

57. Joan Kerr, ed., *Heritage: The National Women's Art Book*, Roseville East, 1995, p.442.

58. Judith McKay, *Ellis Rowan: A Flower-Hunter in Queensland*, Brisbane, 1990, pp.1-2.

59. North painted with Rowan at Albany, Western Australia, and at Derriweit Heights, Rowan's family retreat north-west of Melbourne, where her father had laid out the gardens with advice from his friend, Baron von Mueller, the government botanist in Victoria, who was a correspondent of Von Haast. Rowan described North as: '...the pioneer of my ambition. A world-wide traveller in search of specimens, her description of her adventures was so vivid, so graphic, so thrilling in its prospects of wider fields that I became infected, stimulated by an example and a result beyond dreams successful. Retiring to my room that night, after my

conversation with her, I resolved to do as she had done. I would travel the world in search of flowers rare and wonderful, travel countries inaccessible, as well as those which offered difficulties only imaginary.' 'Ellis Rowan, An Australian Artist's Adventures', *New Idea*, 6 February 1905, p.714, quoted by Judith McKay, *Ellis Rowan: A Flower-Hunter in Queensland*, p.2.; Julie King, 'Flower Hunters in the Colonial Landscape: Contexts and Connections', *Bulletin of New Zealand Art History*, Vol. 17, 1996, pp.13-26.

60. *Argus*, 21 August 1894, p.5. The Art Gallery of New South Wales has no record of the acquisition of a painting by Margaret Stoddart.

61. *Sun*, 31 August 1894, p.4.

62. *Sun*, 5 October 1894, p.9; *Age*, 2 October 1894, p.6.

63. *Press*, 3 September 1894, p.4.

64. R.D.J. Collins, 'Grace Joel and Australia', *Bulletin of New Zealand Art History*, Vol. 14, 1993, pp.29-40.

65. Victoria Hammond and Juliet Peers, *Completing the Picture*, p.49.

66. Dora Meeson Coates, *George Coates: His Art and His Life*, London, 1937, pp.9-10.

67. Letter to Rosa Dixon from Margaret Stoddart, Fendalton, 2 October 1895.

68. On 8 September 1894, the Official Assignee transferred all the Diamond Harbour land that had been sold by the trust to Hawkins back to the trust. Hawkins's total debt to the trust was £7,193 6s 8d (capital £6,600 + £593 6s 8d) [137D 219].

69. E.C. Richards, 23 March 1897, *Diary of E.R. Chudleigh 1862-1921*, Macmillan Brown Library, University of Canterbury.

70. Letter to Rosa Dixon from Frances Hodgkins, Bank N.S. Wales, 1 October 1900. Frances Hodgkins, MS-1016, 1875-1901. National Library of New Zealand, Wellington.

The Making of a Landscapist

Margaret was probably in England early in 1898 and, later that year, she exhibited at the Autumn Exhibition of the Royal Birmingham Society of Artists, where her address was given as c/o Miss Meeson, 9 Hill Road, St John's Wood, London.[1] She spent nine years in Europe, during which time her painting was transformed in its style and by her concentration on landscape themes. Europe gave her the opportunity to increase her skills as a landscapist by working at an artists' colony, and at sketching grounds in France and Italy. She broadened her subject matter so that, from this time on, landscape would exist alongside, and sometimes even overtake, flower painting as the principal theme in her work. This period was important in a number of different ways: she developed her painting techniques, explored a new range of subjects and, released from the constraints of home, she enjoyed greater freedom to work as an artist. Any doubt about her identity as a professional painter was banished by her determined effort to compete in the British art world.

Margaret had acquired some familiarity with the artistic directions she pursued in Europe before leaving New Zealand. Painters from the Newlyn School, including Stanhope Forbes (1857-1947), Frank Bramley (1857-1915), Thomas Gotch (1854-1931), Adrian (1854-1935) and Marianne (1855-1927) Stokes and Norman Garstin (1847-1926) (with whom Margaret, Frances Hodgkins and Dorothy Richmond studied in Europe), exhibited at Dunedin in the 1889-90 New Zealand and South Seas Exhibition. The purchase of Forbes's *Preparations for Market, Quimperlé, Brittany*, 1883, for Dunedin's gallery, and of Adrian Stokes's *Among the Sandhills* by Captain Garsia, a one-time member of the Canterbury Society of Arts, is evidence of local interest in the open-air (*plein-air*) painters of the Newlyn School.[2] In 1889, the arrival in New Zealand of James Nairn (1859-1904), a member of the Scottish Impressionist Glasgow School, followed by the Italian Girolamo Nerli (1860-1926), from Australia, put a younger generation of painters here in touch with recent artistic developments overseas.

Margaret was one of the first members of the Palette Club, an association of Christchurch artists founded in 1889. Its members included Dora Meeson, Rosa Budden and Alfred Wilson Walsh (1859-1919), who had been appointed in 1886 to take the landscape classes at the School of Art, and William Menzies Gibb (1859-1931), who had trained at the end of the 1870s at the National Gallery School in Melbourne. The Palette Club provided a focus for the exploration of new ideas; the group valued broad effects and frequently worked outdoors: 'Sketches…are of peculiar interest, as representing at first hand, the artist's impression of nature; they are his notes, taken when face to face with her, and may, in some instances, afford a truer insight into the impressions produced on his mind at this time than a carefully prepared picture, done when not directly under her influence…'[3] observed one reviewer at their 1890 exhibition. Their exhibition in 1894 consisted mainly of 'outdoor work', which was 'as evident in the finished pictures, of which there is a large proportion, as in the sketches themselves'.[4] It included paintings from around New Zealand, and critics remarked on the importance of art clubs in Auckland, Wellington, Dunedin and Nelson in fostering work from nature. Their adoption of outdoor painting and the value that was placed on the vividness of an impression and broadly worked sketch are evidence of new aesthetic sensibilities in the 1890s. The influence on Margaret's work is seen in *Sumner Beach*, 1893, especially when this is compared with *Canterbury Plains from Dyers Pass Road*, 1888, painted only five years earlier.

Plein-air practice affected both the subject matter and geography of landscape painting. Younger artists avoided picturesque and sublime sites such as Milford and the Sounds: 'We have had quite enough to spare of the Sounds, and Mr Drummond gives us yet another Mitre Peak,' railed the *Press* critic in 1890.[5] The Palette Club organised weekly meetings outdoors and local painters worked in greater numbers at Sumner, the Estuary and New Brighton, accessible sites that were described by their opponents as the 'tit bits of Canterbury scenery, (not the mountains.)'.[6] The *plein-air* movement opened up the way for women to participate increasingly in landscape art, a development that was satirised in a cartoon which appeared in 1900 in the *Triad*.

Margaret's visit to Melbourne in 1894 allowed her to see the Victorian Artists Exhibition, which included work by Jane Sutherland (1855-1928), Clara Southern (1861-1940), May Vale (1862-1945), Walter Withers (1854-1914), John Mather (1848-1916), E. Phillips Fox (1865-1915) and David Davies (1864-1939). The review in the *Argus* remarked on a growing tendency in landscape painting towards 'the realisation of luminous atmospheric effects… and although this method of looking at and interpreting nature owes its first impulse to French example, yet the evidences are many that a distinctly Australian school is in process of formation…'.[7] Margaret's stay also coincided with the foundation by E. Phillips Fox of the first summer school of painting at Charterisville, where students, 'mainly women from well-to-do or professional families' were instructed in outdoor working.[8] In the following year, Margaret's paintings of the Yarra were exhibited at the Palette Club exhibition in 1895, where critics detected a French influence; the works were criticised for their flatness.[9]

PAINTING IN EUROPE 1898-1906

Shortly after her arrival in Europe, Margaret made her base at St Ives in Cornwall, which was home to a group of artists with a commitment to open-air painting. In 1902, Norman Garstin explained that the communities in

Canterbury Plains from Dyers Pass Road, 1888
Watercolour and pencil
270 × 375mm
Collection of Robert McDougall Art Gallery, Christchurch

Sumner Beach, 1893
Watercolour
360 × 520mm
Private Collection

ART.
HE: "That's an awfully jolly bit you're painting. I've a mind to have a shot at it myself."
SHE: "Oh, I didn't know you were an artist."
HE: "Artist! good gracious! I'm not an artist, I only just do the sort of thing you're doing."

A cartoon from the *Triad*, 1 November 1900, p. 11.

Cornwall owed their origins to the dissatisfaction of younger painters with training in Britain in the 1880s, which had led them across the Channel to work at one of the artists' colonies in France. It was there that they learned to value the 'direct inspiration of nature', and the immediacy of their own experience and, after they returned to England, a number of them settled in Cornwall at Newlyn and St Ives,[10] where the special quality of the light had particular appeal:

The western end of Cornwall… has the charming distinction of being between two seas – a southern sea between us and the sun, with the atmosphere over it soft and broken, seen against the light; and a northern sea upon which the sun shines flat, abrupt, positive and dark with colour; distinct in its horizon, its profound blue breaking into fine shining lines of foam. Towards the southern sea there is innumerable shadow. Every particle of the tender English air has its darkened side towards our eyes – shadow perceptible only as a general mystery, not marring the light, rather adding a quality that is more radiant than light. Over the north sea the midsummer sun makes wave and sky look like a vision, or like the heavens and waters of a dream, because the colour is so steady and profound, and we are unaware of the multitudinous atmosphere which is the breath of England. Here we do not see this atmosphere, for the full light is upon it. St Ives stands by this visionary northern water, a little town so hilly and so jostled together that it is almost bound to have some happy accidents of building to take up the suggestions of dips and ascents, climbing pavements, walls clinging to the hill-side, sudden leaps of view from the top of a little street on to the twinkling sea below.[11]

Margaret spoke enthusiastically about the brilliance of the Cornish atmosphere, its rugged coastline, bleak landscape and the contrasting beauty of its fresh green countryside – those aspects of the region that inspired many paintings she completed while living there:

I think there is no place like Cornwall. The atmosphere there is more like that of the South of Europe, and you have most magnificent sea coasts and bleak mining country, which almost reminds one of parts of New Zealand, except for the ruined smoke-stacks. In some districts the aspect of the country is like a garden in spring.[12]

Apple Blossom, (c. 1902-06)
Watercolour and bodycolour over charcoal
435 × 540mm
Collection of Southland Art Gallery Trust Board

The sheltered harbour at St Ives, set within an open bay on the Atlantic coast of West Cornwall, is situated about 16 kilometres from Newlyn, and its sandy beaches and rocky coast, the orchards at nearby St Erth and an expanse of moorland beyond made this a not unfamiliar landscape for Margaret Stoddart. Unlike Newlyn, where artists concentrated mainly on large-scale figure subjects, St Ives was favoured by landscapists, and it became the temporary home to numerous foreign and English painters.[13] Whereas Newlyn faced east, it was the north-east to north-west aspect at St Ives, according to Norman Garstin, which produced a succession of light effects in the bay, making the painting there more 'impressionistic and sensuous in colour'.[14]

The American-born painter, James McNeill Whistler (1834-1903), Walter Sickert (1860-1942) and Mortimer Menpes (1860-1938), an Australian, worked at St Ives in 1883-84, and they were among the colony's first visiting artists. Margaret was possibly the first New Zealander to paint there, although St Ives was certainly well known to Australian artists in the 1890s. Her friendship with Dora Meeson may have taken her there. Dora's relationship with the Australian artist, George Coates (1869-1930), whom she married in London in 1903 after an eight-year courtship, meant that Dora knew a wide circle of Australian painters in Europe; Coates had travelled to England in 1897 with his friend, David Davies, who had painted at St Ives in 1892, and who returned once again to Cornwall. Meeson and Coates were also acquainted with the Melbourne artist, E. Phillips Fox, who had worked at St Ives in the early 1890s.[15] While Margaret was there, the Australian residents included Will Ashton (1881-1963), Hayley Lever (1876-1958) and Louis Grier (1864-1920), with whom she took lessons.[16]

Round the turn of the century, St Ives provided a congenial environment for artists from all over the world. An artists' club founded in 1888 by Louis Grier, and open to male and female members, provided a centre for social life and for the exchange of ideas. Tuition was available from Grier and Julius Olsson (1864-1942), and their classes provided a number of artists with an

Rambling sketches, St Ives, Cornwall.
Illustrated London News, 16 March 1889

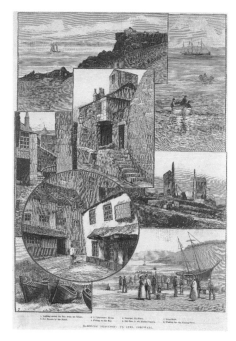

Cyrus Cuneo, *A sketching class at St Ives,
Cornwall.*
Black and White, 25 April 1903

introduction to the colony. Margaret's presence at St Ives is mentioned first in March 1899, when she was a student of Grier, a tonal landscapist and marine painter.[17] She exhibited at the annual show days at St Ives from 1902 to 1904, and in 1906, when 'a large crowd of visitors went through the irregular and quaint courts and streets to the various studios, where the pictures intended for the Academy and other London exhibitions were on view'.[18] Margaret painted on the continent and elsewhere in England, and she probably copied the pattern of artists at St Ives – leaving her studio around late spring, travelling up to London or beyond and then returning to the colony in the following autumn.[19] In 1898 or 1899, she went to Norway and, from paintings that she exhibited in New Zealand, it is known that she visited Switzerland before 1901; in 1902, she was in France.[20] She probably worked in France on more than one occasion, and took lessons there from Charles Lasar, an American artist whose classes catered for the growing numbers of women students arriving from all over the world to study art.[21] She also painted with Norman Garstin, whose sketching trips to the continent began in 1899.[22] Both Frances Hodgkins and Dorothy Richmond were his pupils in 1901. Margaret worked at Étaples, and along the Normandy coast, as well as spending almost a year in Italy in 1905-06, where she stayed at Venice, Rome and Capri.[23]

The prominent resident or visiting artists at St Ives when Margaret worked there included Adrian Stokes, whose painting she saw in New Zealand, Julius Olsson, Moffat Lindner (1852-1949), John Arnesby Brown (1866-1955) and Alfred East (1849-1913), all of whom specialised in landscape and/or marine painting. Charles Marriott, a one-time art critic for the Times, who lived at St Ives from 1901 to 1910, recalled that, in this period, 'Most of the painters then living in St Ives practised the broad impressionism that derives ultimately from Constable, and there were links with Bastien-Lepage, Whistler, Sargent, and the Glasgow School.'[24] The painting that Margaret completed in Europe reveals a variety of influences derived from the many different ways of understanding and interpreting Impressionism in British painting.[25] Those individual artists whom Margaret admired as the 'watercolourists of today' were Frank Brangwyn (1867-1956), Alfred East, an artist whose loyalties lay with Constable, and Arthur Melville (1855-1932) and James Paterson (1854-1932), both members of the Glasgow School, which was known for its adventurous colour and decorative concerns.[26]

Seascapes and harbour views provided the opportunity to explore atmospheric effects and the play of coloured reflections on water, and these were popular themes at St Ives. *The Harbour St Ives* (c. 1902-06), a large-scale watercolour, was shown shortly after Margaret's return to New Zealand, at the Annual Exhibition of the Canterbury Society of Arts in 1907. Its mixture of tonalism enlivened by touches of colour is related to the subdued Impressionism of her teachers in Cornwall, Louis Grier and Norman Garstin,

and to a more innovative use of colour and brushwork, which she could have seen in work by the Glasgow painters.

She concentrated on Impressionist concerns and worked outdoors at different times of the year on a variety of weather effects and seasonal themes. A painting, *Bluebells* (c.1902-06), now in a New Zealand private collection, was shown with the Society of Women Artists in 1906, and at an exhibition of work Margaret held at the Baillie Gallery in July of that year. Woodland scenes and orchards in springtime were established motifs in Impressionist painting, and these were some of her favourite subjects in England. In April 1902, Frances Hodgkins referred to an invitation she had received from Margaret: 'Miss Stoddart wants me to join her at a small village St Erth a few miles from here & paint spring blossoms…'[27] Although Frances chose to remain at Penzance, *Blossom,* signed and dated by Margaret in 1902, was probably painted on her sketching trip to St Erth, only a short train journey from St Ives. This painting is closely related to a small sketch from this time, *Old Cornish Orchard* (c.1902), in which an overall impression is combined with a decorative effect produced by her expressive brushmarks and a

Bluebells, (c.1902-1906)
Watercolour and bodycolour
240 × 340mm
Private Collection

71

vigorous application of opaque bodycolour, representing the profusion of spring blossom.

Margaret painted several versions of this theme, in which she captured an effect of light filtered through blossom trees in an orchard. In *Apple Blossom* (c.1902-06), a more colourful and probably later work, the red roofs of two houses can be glimpsed in full sunlight through the trees. Margaret has worked broadly on the picture as a whole to register how the play of light and shade within the orchard affects both form and colour. The gnarled tree trunks and branches are vigorously outlined in dark paint, and light strokes are interspersed with heavily pronounced ones to recreate the patterned shadows thrown on the ground by a canopy of branches. The handling in *Spring Blossom* (c.1906) is even freer; after a succession of wet washes laid on the paper, a variety of lightly painted strokes have been worked together with touches of bodycolour to capture sunlight and shade and enliven the decorative surface.

Landscape art in the Edwardian period was characterised by a strong sense of nostalgia for the English countryside, and this influenced Margaret's selection of themes for her paintings and their location. The east of England was a favourite region with Alfred East and Arnesby Brown, two frequent

Storm Clouds, Blythburgh, Suffolk,
also known as *Suffolk Village,* (c.1905-06)
Watercolour and bodycolour
255 × 360mm
Collection of Robert McDougall Art Gallery, Christchurch

A Suffolk Lane, also known as *A Surrey Lane,*
(c. 1905-06)
Watercolour and bodycolour over charcoal
240 × 345mm
Collection of Bishop Suter Art Gallery, Nelson

Christmas Roses, 1906
Watercolour and bodycolour
445 × 590mm
Private Collection

visitors to St Ives, and it became one of Margaret's chosen sketching grounds. She described its attractions in an interview in 1907, shortly after her return to New Zealand: 'I am very fond of the East Coast of England. The last two summers I spent in Suffolk and Norfolk. There are in these counties the most old-fashioned places you can possibly imagine. The people won't use reapers and binders. They call them new-fangled notions; and they still grind their corn in the old-fashioned windmills; and then they tell you gravely that farming doesn't pay.'[28] It was probably on a sketching trip in 1905 or 1906 that she painted *A Suffolk Lane*, a picturesque rural scene of a figure making his way along a winding road lined with overgrown grass verges, meandering hedgerows and clumps of trees. The flatness of the East Anglian landscape and its expanse of sky and banked up clouds provided marvellous opportunities for a painter to concentrate on a range of weather effects. *Storm Clouds, Blythburgh, Suffolk* (c.1905-06) shows how she extended her painting techniques during this period. She used the fluency of the watercolour medium and worked with broad brush strokes on wet paper to depict the heavy clouds and approaching storm over the village.

Impressionist concerns are seen in flower paintings from this period, although dating works with certainty is sometimes difficult. *First Flowers of Spring* (c.1902-06), identified by an inscription in pencil on the back of the painting, was shown at the Annual Exhibition of the Canterbury Society of Arts in May 1907. The composition of an arrangement of mixed spring flowers in a vase, placed on a reflective surface against a resonant tonal background, employs a similar format to that used in *Christmas Roses,* which is signed and dated 1906. This was probably first exhibited as *Les roses de Noël* in Paris at the Salon of the Société Nationale des Beaux-Arts in 1906.

The question of when Margaret abandoned precise drawing for more

First Flowers of Spring, also known as *Spring Flowers,*
(c. 1902-06)
Watercolour and bodycolour
382 × 555mm
Collection of Robert McDougall Art Gallery, Christchurch

painterly techniques is complicated by *Apple Blossom*, which is dated 1897, before she is thought to have arrived in England. In the catalogue of her retrospective in 1928, *An Exhibition of Past and Present Work by Miss M.O. Stoddart*, her departure for Europe was given as 1897, but a flower painting at the Canterbury Museum, *Myoporum laetum (Ngaio)*, dated 11 December 1897, as well as her painting of *Lyttelton Harbour*, dated 1898 (Private Collection), puts this timing in some doubt. A shipping notice in the *Lyttelton Times* recorded that the Misses Stoddart and Jones departed on 12 February 1898 on the SS *Wakatipu* for Sydney, in what was probably the first stage of Margaret's voyage to England.

Apple Blossom was one of five works that the artist presented to the Christchurch Technical College for the Memorial Hall to commemorate students who had died in the Great War, and it was probably dated some

Apple Blossom, (c. 1897)
Watercolour and bodycolour
655 x 497mm
Collection of Christchurch Polytechnic, Te Whare
Runanga o Otautahi

years after it was painted. Several of Margaret's works are unsigned or bear more than one signature, which suggests that it was not uncommon for her to sign, and probably date, her paintings some time after they were completed. In terms of its understanding of Impressionist aims, *Apple Blossom* almost certainly dates from when she was in England. The freedom with which she worked, and the placing of complementary touches of yellow on the blue vase, reveal a high degree of confidence. Her sensitivity to the play of light is registered in the depiction of petals, and in her handling of reflections on the table. An harmonious background of blues with warm browns sets off the freshness of the pale flowers, and its effectiveness as a composition is related to the subtlety of her placing the vase slightly right of centre, which complements the balanced arrangement of blossoms and adjustment of colour and tone.

Her approach to composition, and the painterliness and breadth of

Spring Flowers, Cornwall, also known as
Narcissi and White Daffodils, (c. 1902-06)
Watercolour and bodycolour
590 × 465mm
Collection of Robert McDougall Art Gallery, Christchurch

treatment found in her English flower paintings, were related to nineteenth-century French traditions. Henri Fantin-Latour (1836-1904) enjoyed a high reputation in England while Margaret was there. He exhibited at the Royal Academy in 1898-1900, and his work was held by many London dealers.[29] Margaret also visited France and it was in Paris at the Salon, rather than in England, that she preferred to exhibit her flower paintings at this time.

Apple Blossom can be compared with a more complex composition, *Spring Flowers, Cornwall,* (c.1902-06) which was shown at the Annual Exhibition of the Auckland Society of Arts in 1907, and illustrated that year in the *New Zealand Graphic*.[30] English spring flowers were a common theme in Margaret's work before she left New Zealand, and one that she concentrated on during her time away. Its careful floral arrangement, the play of reflections on the table and the contrast between the subdued colours in the background and the freshness of spring flowers, are characteristic of the Impressionist approach that Margaret cultivated in England.

Frances Hodgkins's letters contain several references to Margaret Stoddart, shedding light on the context that they shared as colonial women artists in Europe. While Frances was in Europe from 1901 until 1903, she recorded a number of meetings with Margaret. These prompted some criticisms of her painting, which were balanced by sympathetic reflections about her character and her career. Frances's superior talent was brought to bear sharply on Margaret's work. In 1902, she visited St Ives with Dorothy Richmond, where they looked up Margaret. While conceding that some paintings were 'splendid', Frances believed that she had lost her way: '…her old vigour & freshness has given place to woolliness & want of form – which she seems to have lost in her searching after tones & values. It is the rock on which so many of the Newlyn people have split – they see nothing but tones & they miss everything else.'[31] Frances continued: 'She is a wonderful girl & she tells me she manages to live on £1 a week – I am going over to share her sitting room with her next month when the spring blossom comes out – & St Ives is a paradise of beauty and I shall try & learn the art of keeping down expenses'.[32]

When Frances came across Margaret at Bushey, Hertfordshire, where she was working during the summer in 1903, she described their cramped meetings: '…When Miss Stoddart calls on me I put my head as far out of the window as possible & her feet she disposes of in the fireplace – & so we manage it…'.[33] Yet despite the exhilaration of their new surroundings, times were hard; in 1903, Margaret had spent about five years working in Europe, and she discussed with Frances her painting and future plans:

> I found Miss Stoddart here also & like myself – very disappointed with the country, we both agree that after Cornwall it is a poor place. She has applied for an art teacher's post at a school in Pretoria at a salary of £300 a year and she is hoping daily to hear she has been appointed. I hope so too, it will be a great relief

& rest to have a fixed salary after 5 years precarious struggle with one's brush – she has splendid pluck & is always so cheery & purposeful & un-downcast. I wish her painting had been a greater success – it doesn't seem to have caught on – with all its cleverness & knowledge it just lacks that charm without which good work is so often uninteresting. After our work is over we go for long walks & talks in the evening. She is full of theories and I have none at all, which leaves me all the freer to disagree with hers – she thinks I am suffering from want of teaching & I think her chief fault lies in *too* much teaching – it is so easy to paint like your master & to think other peoples thoughts, the difficulty is to be yourself, assimilate all that is helpful but keep your own individuality, as your most precious possession – it is one's only chance.[34]

Frances respected Margaret's commitment as an artist and evidently enjoyed her company but she remained critical of her painting. She perceived that the essential difference between them stemmed from Margaret's dependence on her teachers, which contrasted sharply with her firm belief in herself. Although Frances's comments possibly reveal more about herself than they do about Margaret, they underline the difficulties that women faced in asserting their individuality, and single-mindedly pursuing their ambition.

When the two women exhibited together in 1902 at the Baillie Gallery in London, Frances had reported home:

…I couldn't grumble seeing I had sold one [painting] for £12.12. Miss Stoddart had hers upstairs in a room by herself – they were only mounted & didn't look their best – poor girl she has had rather bad luck I am afraid – only 4 small £4.4. sold – one of which Miss Richmond had bought… She works so hard – it seems so sad she should be so little appreciated. She got very good Press notices I believe tho' I have not yet seen them.[35]

It was at this exhibition, however, which included work by Grace Joel, Dorothy Richmond and Frances Hodgkins, that Margaret's painting was singled out for praise. A review in the *Sunday Times*, possibly written by Frank Rutter, compared Margaret's painting with Robert Allan and E.A. Waterlow, and promised that she need only to add '…the impressionism of Arthur Melville to go very far indeed, and in her best work there is promise that these further achievements are within her essential gifts'.[36] Melville experimented with the watercolour medium in a way that Frances Hodgkins described as 'at first sight you laugh, then out of a chaos of blots comes wonderful form and colour and you finally end by admiring very much indeed'.[37]

Margaret exhibited widely during nine years away: in 1898 with the Royal Birmingham Society of Artists, in 1899 with the Royal Institute of Painters in Watercolour, London and from 1899 to 1900 with the Royal Society of British Artists, London. Although it was mainly landscapes that she exhibited in England, her flower paintings were accepted at the Salon of the Société des

Artistes Français in 1902-04. From 1905 to 1906 she exhibited in Paris with the more progressive Société Nationale des Beaux-Arts. Before leaving London in 1906, she gained acceptance at the Royal Academy with *A Capri Garden*, painted in 1905 in her more colourful style. Frances Hodgkins reported to her mother: 'I have just heard that I am out of the R.A. this year worst luck. Butler and Miss Stoddart are in though so N.Z. is represented. They say it is a worse than usual bad year & that there is very little good work. Still bad as it is I should like to be there.'[38]

In 1906, Margaret exhibited for the first time with the Society of Women Artists, London, and at the end of June she returned to the Baillie Gallery with an exhibition of almost forty paintings, nearly all of them landscapes. In his review in the *Sunday Times*, Frank Rutter noted briefly: 'Miss M.O.

A Corner of my Garden, (c.1911)
Watercolour and bodycolour over charcoal
320 × 460mm
Private Collection

Stable at Diamond Harbour, (c.1907-13)
Watercolour and bodycolour over charcoal
255 × 355mm
Bradshaw Collection, Canterbury Museum, Christchurch

Landscape with Wood and Sheep, (c.1907-13)
Watercolour and bodycolour
280 × 388mm
Auckland Art Gallery Collection

Stoddart, in her watercolours of Italy and England, emulates more modern artists with more varying success. She is not lacking in dexterity, but should strive for more harmony in her colour effects.'[39] This was the last show of work that she held in England; in November, she returned to New Zealand.

RETURN TO NEW ZEALAND

In an interview in 1907, soon after Margaret's arrival in New Zealand, she made clear that her artistic inclinations lay with the progressive directions in late Victorian and Edwardian art. She confidently allied herself with the painters from Newlyn, St Ives and the Glasgow School, and emphasised that it was French art which gained her admiration during her time away: 'France… is certainly the head-quarters of art. The leading men in Great Britain have studied in Paris and have been influenced by French art. In fact, as I have said, Paris is the head-quarters of all European art, and all students go there. Of course when they return to their native countries their individuality manifests itself; but the best of their training comes from Paris.'[40] Although, in common with many colonial artists in this period, Margaret sought and gained academic approval, she was opposed to the authority of the Royal Academy:

> In many respects I think England is very behind hand. The Academy set is hard to move, and much of the finest work done in the United Kingdom, they will not have there. For instance there is the Glasgow School. Much of the work done by adherents of that school is of world wide fame, yet the Academy will not have it. This set of painters has established a standard in Scotland which has won recognition in all European centres. In the case of a few of the painters of this school, the Royal Academy has been compelled, however, to hang their pictures.[41]

Margaret's painting had been formed initially by the teaching she received as a student at the Canterbury College School of Art, and her encounter with British Impressionism meant representing her perceptions in a new way. She concentrated on the vividness of her impression, which was frequently combined in a painting with her concern for its overall decorative effect. She learned to work freely to capture the colours and tones she perceived in her subject, and to emphasise the marks that she made on the paper.

At the turn of the century in New Zealand, however, her Impressionist painting constituted a radical style. Flower paintings, completed in what the critics called 'her modern style', provoked hostile criticism when they were first exhibited here:

> Time was when Miss M.O. Stoddart was recognised beyond the limits of this colony as a remarkably fine flower painter, and even Mrs Rowan, one of the cleverest artists in this branch whom Australia has known, had nothing but praise for her work. One wishes the same could be said nowadays, but a taste for a woolly misty impressionism has fallen upon her to the detriment of her work… [42]

Critics complained that the great charm of Miss Stoddart's early flower pieces – accuracy and close representation of nature – had been replaced by a 'vagueness or cloudiness of execution…'.[43] Her work came under attack as reviewers around the country, unsympathetic to impressionist effects, took her to task for being untrue to nature: 'It is becoming the fashion, now, to paint flowers as if bathed in a sort of haze, but it is a departure which means a disregard of the natural [illegible] of ordinary vision'.[44]

Nevertheless, it was to be her flower painting, and particularly her depictions of roses, which gradually restored her reputation after her return. She showed two paintings of roses at the Annual Exhibition of the Canterbury Society of Arts in 1908, and again in 1909 and in 1910. In 1909, a photograph of the artist appeared in the *Weekly Press* under the heading, 'A successful New Zealand artist Miss M.O. Stoddart'; the accompanying caption reported her acceptance at the Salon, where she had exhibited 2851, *Les Roses* and 2852, *Les Roses*.[45] Three years later, the Canterbury Society of Arts purchased *Anna Ollivier Roses* (c.1912) for 9 guineas from its annual exhibition in 1912. These events went some way towards securing her success and in 1912 the *Press* critic remarked that 'The work of Miss M.O. Stoddart is above all poetical in feeling. She has a broad impressionist outlook that is very satisfying…'.[46]

As well as being Margaret's favourite floral motif throughout her life, the rose has been described in New Zealand gardening history as the plant that was held 'in the greatest esteem in the earliest decades of this century'.[47] It enjoyed enormous prestige throughout the country and especially in Christchurch, which took an early lead in nineteenth-century rose growing.[48] (This may have been related to the loyalty the city felt towards its English

A SUCCESSFUL NEW ZEALAND ARTIST: MISS M. O. STODDART.

Miss Stoddart recently received information from the Director of the Salon de la Societe des Artistes Francais, stating that the two pictures sent by her to Paris have been accepted for exhibition in the Salon. — H. H. Clifford.

Photograph of Margaret Stoddart in the Weekly Press, 9 June 1909.
Canterbury Public Library, Christchurch

Anna Ollivier Roses, (c.1912)
Watercolour and bodycolour
395 × 540mm
Collection of Robert McDougall Art Gallery, Christchurch

M.O. Stoddart, *In the rose garden*, (c. 1916).
Catalogue of the Annual Exhibition of the Canterbury Society of
Arts, 1916

Roses, also known as *Roses (White)*, (c.1924)
Watercolour and charcoal
393 × 570mm
Collection of the Museum of New Zealand Te Papa
Tongarewa
Gift of the New Zealand Academy of Fine Arts, 1936
Negative no. B041185

Roses, also known as *Roses (Red)*, (c. 1930)
Watercolour and bodycolour
561 × 782mm
Collection of the Museum of New Zealand Te Papa
Tongarewa
Negative no. B038709

origins.) By the early 1900s New Zealand was well on the way towards making a name for itself in rose-growing culture. New Zealand's first public rose garden was established in Christchurch in 1910, and it soon became a focus for civic pride.[49] Within twenty years a formal rose garden was to be found in every city and main town in the country. Margaret's painting, *In the Rose Garden*, was exhibited in 1916 at the annual exhibitions of the art societies in Christchurch and Wellingon and, almost ten years later, at the Dominions Court of the British Empire Exhibition at Wembley, in England.[50]

The hostility towards Margaret's Impressionist painting gradually diminished and by 1918 a few appreciative comments about her work appeared each year in the reviews of annual exhibitions: 'Miss M.O. Stoddart's pictures are always eagerly looked for. Her reputation as a painter of flowers is solidly upheld by two exceedingly nice studies of roses, quite in her best style.'[51] Margaret Stoddart and Dorothy Richmond were now recognised as the two artists who had established a place for themselves in a category of painting that was frequently undervalued, and invariably overlooked, in preference for landscape: 'It is perhaps a matter for regret that no less than one-fifth of the pictures hung in the main gallery downstairs are "still-life" subjects – many the inevitable zinnias, marigolds, or hydrangeas... Artists like Miss D.K. Richmond or Miss M.O. Stoddart, to mention only a couple out of several, can and do make real pictures out of their still-life subjects.'[52] They were joined by Alfred O'Keeffe (1858-1941) and, in the early 1920s, an understanding of Impressionist aims and techniques led to an appreciation of flower painting as a virtuoso display of an artist's technique, and handling of colour and tone: 'No other work is so relentless in showing up false tone, or faulty form. In addition to this the poetic scope of a study of still life is necessarily so restricted, that to achieve anything higher than a purely decorative effect is extremely difficult. That it may be done has often been proved to us by Miss Stoddart's flower pieces, and in the present exhibition... by O'Keeffe.'[53]

Their decorative charm and modest dimensions contributed to the popularity of Margaret's flower paintings in middle- and upper-class homes, and they seem to have been especially appreciated by female patrons. *Violets* was one of several paintings owned by Mrs Alison MacGibbon, whose interest in Margaret's work went back to her youth in the 1920s, when she was a neighbour of the artist in Christchurch;[54] in 1976, Alison MacGibbon bequeathed her collection of paintings, including *Violets*, to the University of Canterbury; *Camellias* belonged to Mrs Kathleen Kirkby, the daughter of Sir Robert and Lady Anderson, who gifted it to the Anderson Park Gallery in 1992; *Bowl of Roses* was bequeathed by Miss Maude Isabella Mary Haines to the Dunedin Public Art Gallery; and *First Flowers of Spring* was bequeathed, with *Spring Flowers, Cornwall*, to the Robert McDougall Art Gallery by the Christchurch florist, Dorothy Feaver. The council of the New Zealand Academy of

Fine Arts, which included Dorothy Richmond, acquired two flower paintings by Margaret Stoddart. In 1924, the academy purchased *Roses*, also known as *Roses (White)* from its annual exhibition, and this was followed by *Roses*, also known as *Roses (Red)*, which was bought from the annual exhibition in 1930. Flower painting was prominent at every art society exhibition in New Zealand and formed part of this country's cultural tradition.

FLOWERS INTO LANDSCAPE

Back in New Zealand, Margaret was able to apply the painterly techniques and ideas about art that she acquired in Europe to the representation of her surroundings at home and, soon after she returned, she completed a succession of impressionist scenes painted at Diamond Harbour, Sumner and New Brighton. In 1907, she returned to the big house at Diamond Harbour, where she lived with her mother, Anna, and her sisters, Mary and Agnes. In 1908, her brother, John, arrived from Rhodesia for Mary's wedding to Richard Farques Farmer on 4 September at Holy Trinity, Lyttelton and, for a short time at least, the whole family was at Diamond Harbour. After their marriage, Mary and her husband, Richard, went to live at the Stoddarts' old cottage. In the following year, at the age of forty, Mary became pregnant but

Violets

Watercolour and bodycolour

380 × 560mm

W.S. & Alison MacGibbon Collection, University of Canterbury, Christchurch

Camellias

Watercolour and bodycolour

460 × 615mm

Collection of Anderson Park Art Gallery Society Inc. Invercargill

Godley House, Diamond Harbour, (c. 1913)
Watercolour and bodycolour over charcoal
382 × 505mm
Collection of Robert McDougall Art Gallery, Christchurch

Diamond Harbour, 1909
Watercolour and bodycolour over charcoal
255 × 355mm
Collection of Christchurch Civic Art Gallery Trust

The Old Almond Tree, Diamond Harbour
Watercolour and bodycolour over charcoal
235 × 340mm
W.S. & Alison MacGibbon Collection, University of
Canterbury, Christchurch

she died several days after giving birth to a daughter, Frances Mary Stoddart Farques Farmer, on 16 October, and was buried at Lyttelton on 22 October. Margaret's original intention, reported in the press in 1907, had been 'to remain in New Zealand for a year or two',[55] but this plan may well have been changed by the distress of her sister's death and the arrival of the baby. Margaret remained at Diamond Harbour with her mother and Agnes to help with the upbringing of the child. Anna died two years later, in 1911, aged seventy-six, and in 1913 Margaret and Agnes moved to Christchurch, where they continued to care for their niece.

It was during her years at Diamond Harbour that Margaret produced some of her most memorable images, completing a succession of paintings of places that had been familiar since childhood – the old wharf, the farm, fruit trees and the orchard, and the cottage that her father had brought from Australia before his marriage, and where she was born. The country cottage was a popular and nostalgic theme in late Victorian and Edwardian art and, in New Zealand, it symbolised the pioneering years of European settlement. In October 1911, Margaret organised an exhibition of fifty of her paintings at the Canterbury Society of Arts Gallery, where one critic noted: 'One of the most marked features of the exhibition was that the paintings dealt largely – mainly in fact – with Diamond Harbour, where the artist's father had settled in 1851, when the pioneers laid the foundation of the Canterbury settlement'.[56] The reviewer outlined the range of subjects in the show: '…the old homestead has evidently been one of Miss Stoddart's favourite resorts… A spreading almond tree in full bloom is shown in one picture, and in others there are trees which must have been planted soon after the settlement of Canterbury began, and which have found at Diamond Harbour good soil and a congenial climate.'[57]

In 1911, the year of Margaret's exhibition, Diamond Harbour faced the prospect of future development. The borough of Lyttelton was considering the possibility of purchasing the Diamond Harbour Estate from the Stoddart trust with a view to expanding the port and establishing a suburb to provide housing for the workers at Lyttelton.[58] Councillors and ratepayers were divided over the scheme and, on 16 March 1912, the mayor organised a picnic to Diamond Harbour to view the estate. Edward Chudleigh recorded the events that day:

> Mabel, Edie, and I went to Diamond Harbour to see Marjorie [Margaret] Stoddart. The Mayor of Lyttelton was giving a free treat to all that liked to go from Lyttelton to the Stoddarts just for the public to see how nice it was. The Harbour Board or one of the Boards contemplate buying the property and the purchase has to rest with the ratepayers. The Stoddart gardens are lovely and should not have been entered but hundreds of the public rushed the grounds and stole all they could carry. I never saw anything like it, a disgrace to civilisation.[59]

In 1913, Frances and Margaret Stoddart, who had become the trustees of the Stoddart trust, sold the estate at Diamond Harbour to the Lyttelton Borough Council for the sum of £7,000. Around the time of her departure, Margaret completed a picture of her family home, *Godley House, Diamond Harbour* (c.1913), painted in a similar style to *Old Homestead, Diamond Harbour* (c.1913), which was shown at the Canterbury Society of Arts Exhibition in 1913. The image of the old cottage, overgrown with flowers in the height of summer, evokes a feeling of nostalgia for the past.

Old Homestead, Diamond Harbour, (c.1913)
Watercolour and bodycolour over charcoal
250 × 350mm
Private Collection

Old Homestead, Diamond Harbour, (c.1913)
Watercolour and bodycolour over charcoal
383 × 494mm
Collection of Robert McDougall Art Gallery, Christchurch

A Garden, Cashmere Hills, (c.1915)
Watercolour and bodycolour over charcoal
370 × 490mm
Private Collection

The Drive in Summer
Watercolour and bodycolour over charcoal
245 x 355mm
Private Collection

Above: ***Blossom, Worcester St Bridge***
Watercolour and bodycolour over charcoal
255 x 346mm
Collection of Robert McDougall Art Gallery, Christchurch

Riverside, Autumn, also known as *Autumn River Scene,* and
Autumn, (c. 1930)
Watercolour and charcoal on paper on tan cardboard
461 x 583mm
Collection of the Museum of New Zealand Te Papa
Tongarewa
Negative no. B037388

The move to Christchurch, first to Dublin Street in the central city and then in 1914 to Hackthorne Road in Cashmere, allowed Margaret to develop a range of subjects that she found in her new surroundings, including public parks and suburban gardens, which were established themes in French Impressionist art and in British painting in the late Victorian and Edwardian period. In New Zealand such images represented the progress of European settlement early this century. The parks and gardens of Christchurch were celebrated features of the city, contributing to the creation of its local identity. The *Cyclopedia of New Zealand* boasted in 1903: 'As to flower gardens, every stranger who visits Christchurch is at once struck with the amazing number and beauty of the gardens attached to private dwellings. The level fertile ground, and the large area of the city afford room for horticulture to an extent impossible in Auckland, Wellington, or Dunedin.'[60]

The Jubilee celebrations for Canterbury in 1900, followed by the New Zealand International Exhibition, held at Hagley Park from 1906 to 1907, which attracted almost two million visitors, prompted a sense of pride in the achievements of the Canterbury pioneers and in the appearance of the city. Deprived of the picturesque natural advantages of the other main centres, Christchurch prided itself on the transformation of a flat expanse of swamp and tussock into a city of established parks and gardens. Its parks and reserves and the borders of the Avon River had been planted with different varieties of English trees, whose seasonal changes provided Margaret and other Impressionist artists with a wealth of autumn and spring themes. Slightly further afield, only an hour's tram-ride away, were the seaside resorts at Sumner and New Brighton. In 1903, the *Cyclopedia*

reported that 'On Saturdays, and public holidays, the tramcars are generally crowded with visitors, who have taken "a day off" to spend it in recuperative recreation at Sumner'.[61] Margaret had painted here in the 1890s and from 1916, when she exhibited *The Almond Tree, Clifton, Sumner,* (c.1916) at the Otago Art Society Annual Exhibition (and in the following year at the Annual Exhibition of the Canterbury Society of Arts), she worked there regularly. Well into the 1920s, Sumner, the Estuary and New Brighton provided Margaret with a variety of subjects.

The lessons she had learned in Europe were applied to painting very different places, which she explored in a range of watercolour techniques. In *Bush Fire, Paraparaumu,* (c.1908), the results of working abroad are seen in the tonal washes that are used to capture the effect of thick smoke from the fire and the destruction of the bush. *Sheep Country* (c.1916), which was chosen for reproduction in a section on New Zealand art in the special 1917 *Studio* edition of the *Art of the British Empire Overseas*, also demonstrates her skill in capturing atmospheric effects.[62]

Margaret worked continuously as an artist from the time of her return to New Zealand in 1907 until her death in 1934, and her painting described the diversity of the Canterbury landscape and its varied vegetation: suburban gardens in full bloom, seasonal changes along the Avon, yellow lupins along the New Brighton coastline, the native bush at Otira, images of dry shingle and tussock in the Mackenzie Basin. Her move to the Cashmere Hills, in 1914, provided her with a very different experience of landscape overlooking the Canterbury Plains and the distant Alps beyond and, from the 1920s, her pictorial preferences moved increasingly towards what were seen as characteristic themes within a local landscape tradition. Particular subjects, like

An excursion to Sumner.
Canterbury Museum, Christchurch

Above: **The Almond Tree, Clifton, Sumner,** (c. 1916)
Watercolour and bodycolour over charcoal
255 × 357mm
Collection of Waikato Museum of Art and History,
Te Whare Taonga o Waikato, Hamilton

The Estuary
Watercolour
245 × 345mm
Private Collection

certain sites, have broad cultural associations, and her representation of the shingly riverbeds and dry mountain streams in the South Island Alpine regions were seen to capture the distinctive character of the place.

In Christchurch, James Shelley was the critic who began to nurture the idea of a national art and by the late 1920s, he was drawing attention to those aspects of Margaret's painting that captured the starkness of the New Zealand landscape:

She surprises us anew every year in her strong and biting grip on the essentials of things. In her landscapes she has long thrown aside the search for prettiness and has evolved for herself a method by which the very primeval elements of

Bridge over the Kowhai, (c.1920-c.1930)

Watercolour and bodycolour over charcoal

450 × 485mm

Collection of the Christchurch Polytechnic, Te Whare

Runanga o Otautahi

nature seem to be laid bare – the very stones seem instinct with a life and purpose of their own; as witness the sleeping strength of the river-bed in 'In the Otira,' and the threatening river-bed in 'Mt Rolleston from Arthur's Pass'; or the giants of snow and ice in the Salon picture 'Franz Josef Glacier'; and the living shadows in 'Sandhills.' Arthur's Pass is the truest rendering of this well-known spot we have seen – the cottages here do not look, as they most often do in pictures, as if they had been placed there to provide a picturesque point of foreground interest – Miss Stoddart has plainly set down the inglorious shacks as they really are and given us the feeling of this crude and puny encroachment of man upon the preserves of Nature's majesty. [63]

Describing her work at the Annual Exhibition of the Canterbury Society of Arts in 1934, Shelley maintained: 'Miss Stoddart gives us the true spirit of the shingle-rivers and desolate beaches that must have entered into the very blood of her forbears [sic] when they arrived here'.[64]

In the Mackenzie Country (c.1930) reveals the ability she developed in her later work to reduce the landscape to a few basic elements. She uses a forceful composition in which the boulders and tussock in the foreground are juxtaposed with a distant range of mountains that stretch across the wide Mackenzie Basin in the background. In Allen Curnow's review of Canterbury art in 1950, he declared that this painting was one of only two works that he thought worthy of preserving in what was then a largely British and Victorian collection at the Robert McDougall Art Gallery: 'Somewhat apart, a painter

Rough Creek, Arthur's Pass, exhibited at the Annual Exhibition of the New Zealand Academy of Fine Arts in 1930.
Art in New Zealand, Vol. VIII, No. 2, December 1935

In the Mackenzie Country, (c.1930)

Watercolour and bodycolour over charcoal

480 × 625mm

Collection of Robert McDougall Art Gallery, Christchurch

both older and more intimately Canterbury's, was the late Margaret Stoddart. One landscape and example of her flower-painting are among the handful of pictures worth preserving in the shabby little assortment of the McDougall Gallery, Christchurch's only permanent collection: a pale range that might be a frontier of Erewhon; a panel of clematis disposed by some insight into the behaviour of the flowers.'[65]

No letters or diaries, and very few photographs, have come to light to illuminate Margaret's later years as an artist in New Zealand. She was one of the first members of the Canterbury Women's Club, founded in 1913, a vice-president of the Society for Imperial Culture, and a vice-president of the Canterbury Society of Arts from 1931 until her death in 1934. She was also a member of the Christchurch Sketch Club, and many years later Toss Woollaston vividly remembered her in Christchurch during the early 1930s:

The only criticism I can still remember (not of my work) was by Miss Stoddart, an elderly artist whose watercolour of *Lyttelton Harbour* I had seen (and liked) in the Suter Gallery in Nelson. She took students to task for not using easels –

she had seen a whole landscape class on the banks of the Avon, and not one easel among them. How *could* they paint, with the sky reflected in their work? And she criticised one student's painting for looking as if it had all been painted with the same brush. You should vary your brush-strokes so that, even if you had used only one brush, it didn't look like it.[66]

Margaret was also remembered with some affection by Evelyn Page, who had known her when she was embarking on her career as an artist:

She [Margaret] came to the house many times after my father died. A real stalwart to me. I'm very ashamed that I was not more perceptive to her work. She was a

Cabbage Trees, Clarence Valley, Kaikoura
Watercolour and bodycolour over charcoal
455 x 530mm
Collection of Christchurch Civic Art Gallery Trust

wonderful human being and especially to the young. She gave private lessons at her house in Hackthorne Road. She had a face like a Persian cat: a great big mouth and a short face. She used to wear hats that we all laughed at. The young are so cruel. We were fond of Margaret Stoddart but she was more or less a figure of fun. We all suffered from our Victorian parents and she was lumped in with that. (I am absolutely certain that was why we started the 1927 Group. It was necessary to have somewhere to get out of the Victorian atmosphere.) What she did for me was absolutely wonderful. I clung to her too.[67]

Starting out in the 1880s, Margaret was the first in a line of women watercolourists in Canterbury and, during her later years, she painted with her old friend, Rosa Spencer Bower (formerly Dixon), her daughter, Olivia, and with Cora Wilding and Esther Hope. In 1920, she worked at Mount Ruapehu with Dorothy Richmond.[68]

View of Mount Cook
Watercolour and bodycolour over charcoal
508 × 457mm
Collection of the Museum of New Zealand,
Te Papa Tongarewa. Negative no. B041177

Margaret Stoddart was visiting Hanmer when she died of a heart attack on 10 December 1934; she was sixty-nine years old. Her funeral was held at St Augustine's Church on the Cashmere Hills near her home and she was buried two days later at Bromley Cemetery.

After Margaret's death, James Shelley and Sydney Thompson paid tribute, in an article published in the recently founded periodical, *Art in New Zealand*, to the contribution she had made to the development of painting in her own country:

> For half a century Miss Stoddart gave a guiding hand to the art life of the community, for it was as long ago as 1885 that she was elected to the Council of the Canterbury Society of Arts, which she joined in 1883. She was ever ready to give her time and energy without stint to further the Society's cause, and her name will go down as one of the great battlers for true art in the consolidating period of Canterbury's development… Miss Stoddart was one of the best painters of the Newlyn school, but she had a very individual and independent vision which makes it unsatisfactory to think of her as belonging very definitely to any particular school. Her work, as her character, was very decisive, without being hard or lacking in resilience. Her personality and her painting were one, and the environment in which she was working seemed to identify its spirit with hers. The words of Zola in one of his most famous books – '*Dans l'oeuvre d'art je cherche, j'aime, l'homme, l'artiste,*' apply very fully to Miss Stoddart's work. Her paintings were intimately personal, and in them her very way of life was expressed; they were fine because she was fine, and the deliberate composition and firm technique spoke truly of the high principles and clearly defined character of the woman. Unyielding truth to herself and what she regarded as highest in art was the keynote in her work, and if there is one word that might sum it up it is the word 'integrity'.[69]

About thirty years later, Rita Angus would acknowledge the influence of Margaret's work on her own flower painting. Although Margaret Stoddart was born forty-three years before Angus, she shared with her a delight in the natural world, the local landscape and its diverse and distinctive flora. When Gordon Brown was working on *The Introduction to New Zealand Painting* in the 1960s, his suggestion to Angus that she had been influenced by Dürer provoked a sharp and unequivocal response: 'Your words "Durer's approach to the subject." Leave out please …I never saw a Durer watercolour overseas, and I did not go to Germany… stick to my being a N.Z.er and the limitations. It was Miss Stoddart's watercolours that impressed me when a Canterbury Art Student and later the watercolours at the Turnbull Library, Wellington.'[70]

Margaret Stoddart painting outdoors.
Robert McDougall Art Gallery, Christchurch

Notes:

1. 'Miss Stoddard [*sic*] has gone Home to study, and we shall look forward to great things on her return.' Unreferenced review, dated May 1898, of the Annual Exhibition of the South Canterbury Society of Arts. South Canterbury Society of Arts records, Aigantighe Art Gallery, Timaru; Royal Birmingham Society of Artists 72nd Autumn Exhibition, 1898.

2. Adrian Stokes's painting was purchased from Captain Garsia by the Canterbury Society of Arts in 1902. 13 September 1902, CSA Minute Book 3, Robert McDougall Art Gallery, Christchurch.

3. *Lyttelton Times*, 2 October 1890, p.3.

4. *Lyttelton Times*, 4 September 1894, p.6.

5. *Press*, 1 October 1890, p.6.

6. *Press*, 21 July 1893, p.3.

7. *Argus*, 25 October 1894, p.4.

8. Ruth Zubans, *E. Phillips Fox: His Life and Art*, Carlton, Victoria, 1995, p.85.

9. ' "On the Yarra", a clump of gum trees is the best of the latter, all of which are noticeable as indicating the influence of the French School…', *Lyttelton Times*, 28 June 1895, p.5; 'Miss Stoddart is not successful in her landscapes. There is a flatness about them… In her own department, flowers, Miss Stoddart is as good as ever…' *Lyttelton Times*, 10 October 1895, p.3.

10. Norman Garstin, 'Introduction to the exhibition of Artists and St Ives and Newlyn', Whitechapel Art Gallery, London, 1902, in Tom Cross, *The Shining Sands: Artists in Newlyn and St Ives 1880-1930,* Cambridge, 1994, pp.16-17.

11. Alice Meynell, 'Newlyn', *Art Journal,* 1889, pp.97-102.

12. 'Art in Europe', *Press*, 11 February 1907, p.8.

13. Caroline Fox and Francis Greenacre, *Painting in Newlyn 1880-1930*, Barbican Art Gallery, London, 1985, pp.8-9; Tom Cross, *The Shining Sands*, p.85.

14. Norman Garstin, writing as N.G. in *The Studio*, Vol. VI, No. 33, December 1895, quoted in Tom Cross, *The Shining Sands*, p.85.

15. Ruth Zubans, *E. Phillips Fox* pp.43-51; *Dora Meeson and George Coates*, Jim Alexander Gallery, East Malvern, Victoria, 1984. I am indebted to Myra Scott for this reference.

16. Marion Whybrow, *St Ives 1883-1993: Portrait of an Art Colony,* Woodbridge, Suffolk, 1994, pp.21-108.

17. 'St Ives Artists and their Pictures', *St Ives Weekly Summary*, 25 March 1899.

18. 'St Ives Artists and their Pictures' [from the *Cornishman*], *St Ives Weekly Summary*, 26 March 1904; Margaret Stoddart is mentioned as an exhibitor in the *St Ives Weekly Summary* for these years.

19. Louis Grier, 'A Painter's Club', *The Studio*, Vol. V, 1895, pp.110-112.

20. Margaret exhibited 120, *Fredricksroern* and 134, *A Norwegian Fiord* at the Annual Exhibition of the Canterbury Society of Arts in March 1900; she exhibited 139, *By Lake Lucerne Autumn* at the Annual Exhibition of the New Zealand Academy of Fine Arts in September 1901; *Camiero, France*, which was purchased by the Canterbury Society of Arts in 1905, was dated 1902 by the artist.

21. Charles Lasar is known to have worked in Paris and at Concarneau. Michael Jacobs, *The Good and Simple Life: Artists Colonies in Europe and America*, Oxford, 1985, pp.74-75 and p.82.

22. Garstin also opened 'The Newlyn and Penzance Art School'. Tom Cross, *The Shining Sands*, p.77-78; a reference to the school appears for the first time in 1905 in *The Year's Art*, London.

23. Paintings of Étaples, the Normandy coast, Capri, Venice and Rome were exhibited in New Zealand; 'Art in Europe', *Press*, 11 February 1907, p.8.

24. Quoted by Denys Val Baker, *Britain's Art Colony by the Sea*, London, 1959, p.29.

25. Kenneth McConkey, *Impressionism in Britain*, Ex. Cat. Barbican Art Gallery, London, 1995.

26. 'Art in Europe', *Press*, 11 February 1907, p.8.

27. Letter to Rachel Hodgkins from Frances Hodgkins, 1 Wellington Terrace, Penzance, 13 April 1902. Linda Gill, ed., *Letters of Frances Hodgkins*, Auckland, 1993, p.125.

28. 'Art in Europe', *Press*, 11 February 1907, p.8.

29. Elisabeth Hardouin-Fugier and Étienne Grafe, *French Flower Painters of the Nineteenth Century: A Dictionary*, ed. Peter Mitchell, London, 1989, pp.45-50.

30. *New Zealand Graphic*, 4 May 1907, p.6.

31. Letter from Frances Hodgkins [Penzance], 27th March[1902], Gill, pp.122-123.

32. *Ibid.*

33. Letter to Rachel Hodgkins from Frances Hodgkins, 2 Rudolph Terrace, Bushey, Herts., 11 June 1903. Gill, p.166.

34. *Ibid.*, p.165.

35. Letter to Rachel Hodgkins from Frances Hodgkins, 24 Gordon Place W. [London], 23rd Oct. [1902]. Gill, p.141.

36. *Sunday Times*, 12 October 1902, p.6.

37. E.H. McCormick, 'Frances Hodgkins: The Path to Impressionism: 1892-1912', *Art New Zealand*, 16, p.30.

38. Letter to Rachel Hodgkins from Frances Hodgkins, Casa Frollo, Venice, 10 May 1906. Gill, p.188.

39. Frank Rutter, 'Mr Baillie's Discoveries', *Sunday Times*, 1 July 1906, p.12.

40. 'Art in Europe', *Press*, 11 February 1907, p.8.

41. *Ibid*.

42. *Press*, 16 April 1902, p.8.

43. *Press*, 4 April 1903, p.5.

44. *New Zealand Times*, 13 October 1911, p.4., in New Zealand Academy of Fine Arts Exhibitions 1920-1937 Clippings Book p.20. Alexander Turnbull Library, National Library, Wellington.

45. *Weekly Press*, 9 June 1909, p.40; I would like to acknowledge the generosity of Roger Collins in making available a list of works exhibited at the Salon of the Société des Artistes Français and of the Société Nationale des Beaux-Arts.

46. *Press*, 26 March 1912, p.7.

47. Thelma Strongman, *The Gardens of Canterbury*, Wellington, 1984, p.143.

48. Keith Stewart, *Rosa Antipodes: the History of Roses in New Zealand*, Auckland, 1994, p.109.

49. *Ibid*., p.125.

50. 'New Pictures for Wembley', *Bulletin of the National Art Association of New Zealand*, Wellington, Nos 2-3, February-March 1925, p.9.

51. *Press*, 19 March 1918, p.8.

52. *Evening Post* , 25 September 1931, p.3.

53. G.M. Lester, 'Notice 111', *Press*, 28 March 1925, p.110.

54. Julie King, *A Private View: Pictures from The W.S. & Alison MacGibbon Collection*, Ex. Cat., School of Fine Arts, University of Canterbury, Christchurch, 1995.

55. 'Art in Europe', *Press*, 11 February 1907, p.8.

56. *Lyttelton Times*, 24 October 1911, p.5.

57. *Ibid*; when *Old Homestead, Diamond Harbour* (c.1913) was exhibited at the Annual Exhibition of the Canterbury Society of Fine Arts in 1913, the *Lyttelton Times* noted that her painting recalled '…the days when workers' villages were not dreamt of, and when family cottages seemed to have a more homely and picturesque air than they have in these days of lathe-and-plaster walls, tiled roofs and electrically lighted rooms'. *Lyttelton Times*, 14 March 1913, p.11.

58. Mary Stapylton-Smith, *Diamond Harbour: Portrait of a Community*, Diamond Harbour, 1993, pp.38-39.

59. 16 March 1912, *Diary of E.R. Chudleigh 1862-1921.*

60. *The Cyclopedia of New Zealand*, Wellington, 1897-1908, Vol. 3 Canterbury Provincial District, p.47.

61. *Ibid*., p.405.

62. E.A.S. Killick, 'Landscape Art in New Zealand', in *Art of the British Empire Overseas*, ed. Charles Holme, *The Studio*, London, 1917, p.105.

63. *Art in New Zealand*, Vol. I, No. 4, June 1929, p.264.

64. J. Shelley, 'CSA Annual Exhibition', Art in New Zealand, Vol.VI, No. 4, June 1934, p.180.

65. Allen Curnow, 'Painting in Canterbury', *New Zealand Listener*, 8 December 1950, p.8; Brassington file, Robert McDougall Art Gallery, Christchurch.

66. Toss Woollaston, *Sage Tea*, Auckland, 1980, p.219.

67. Evelyn Page, quoted in Janet Paul & Neil Roberts, *Evelyn Page: Seven Decades,* Robert McDougall Art Gallery, 1986, p.24.

68. *Dominion*, 22 May 1920, p.4, cited in Louis Robert Le Vaillant Johnston, Dorothy Kate Richmond 1861-1935, unpublished MA thesis, University of Auckland, 1991, p.167.

69. Sydney L. Thompson and J. Shelley, 'Miss M.O. Stoddart', *Art in New Zealand,* Vol. VIII, No. 2, December 1935, pp.97-101.

70. Letter to Gordon Brown from Rita Angus, 194a Sydney Street West, Wellington, N.1, 1 May 1968. Rita Angus MS Papers 1399, 1:4, Alexander Turnbull Library, National Library of New Zealand, Wellington.

Paintings in the Exhibition
Flowers into Landscape: Margaret Stoddart 1865-1934

Key: * touring   + Christchurch and Auckland venues only

*1. Alpine Flowers from North Otago (Herpolirion novae zealandiae), 1886
Watercolour and bodycolour on dull green paper, 270 × 355mm
Signed and dated lower right: Herpolirion Novae Zealandiae M.O.S. 1886
Exhibition: CSA Annual 1886, 108 Alpine Flowers from N. Otago (Herpolirion novae zealandiae) £4 4s; OAS Annual 1886 259 Alpine Flowers from North Otago (Herpolirion Novae Zealandiae) £4 4s
Canterbury Museum, Christchurch

*2. Alectryon excelsum (Titoki), 1886
Watercolour and bodycolour over traces of pencil on dull green paper, 355 × 270mm
Signed and dated lower right: Ti Toki Berries M.O.S. 1886
Canterbury Museum, Christchurch

3. Hoheria lyalli (Ribbonwood), 1890
Watercolour and bodycolour over traces of pencil on buff paper, 270 × 375mm
Signed and dated lower right: M.O.S. 31/12/90
Canterbury Museum, Christchurch

4. Hebe salicifolia (Koromiko), 1896
Watercolour and bodycolour over traces of pencil on grey buff paper, 360 × 270mm
Signed and dated lower right: M.O. Stoddart 26/12/96
Canterbury Museum, Christchurch

5. Celmisia coriacea *(Mountain Daisy)*, 1897
Watercolour and bodycolour over traces of pencil on grey buff paper, 355 × 270mm
Signed and dated lower right: M.O. Stoddart 5/1/97
Canterbury Museum, Christchurch

*6. Corokia macrocarpa *(Chatham Islands Korokio)*, 1886
Watercolour and bodycolour over traces of underdrawing on dull green paper, 360 × 270mm
Signed and dated lower right: M.O.S. 7/30/86
Exhibition: CSA An Exhibition of Past and Present Work by Miss M.A. Stoddart, 1928,
80 Corokia macrocarpa
Canterbury Museum, Christchurch

7. Myrsine chathamica *(Chatham Islands Matipo)*, 1886
Watercolour and bodycolour over traces of pencil on buff paper, 360 × 270mm
Signed and dated lower right: M.O.S. 5/8/86
Canterbury Museum, Christchurch

8. Pseudopanax chathamicum *(Chatham Islands Lancewood)*, 1886
Watercolour and bodycolour over traces of pencil on buff paper, 360 × 270mm
Signed and dated lower right: M.O.S. August 20th 1886
Canterbury Museum, Christchurch

9. Pimelea arenaria *(Sand Daphne)* **and Geranium traversii**
  (Chatham cranesbill), 1886
Watercolour and bodycolour over traces of pencil on buff paper, 270 × 375mm
Signed and dated lower right: M.O.S. Nov 22nd 1886
Canterbury Museum, Christchurch

10. Senecio huntii *(Rautini)*, 1886
Watercolour and bodycolour over traces of pencil on buff paper, 355 × 270mm
Signed and dated lower right: M.O.S. Dec 31st 1886
Canterbury Museum, Christchurch

*11. Veronica chathamica (now known as *Hebe chathamica*) **and Calystegia
   soldanella** (*Sand Convolvulus*), 1887
Watercolour and bodycolour over traces of pencil on dull green paper, 270 × 375mm
Signed and dated lower right: M.O.S. Jan 3rd 1887
Canterbury Museum, Christchurch

*12. Moriori Tree Carving, Chatham Islands, also known as *Carved Trees, Chatham
   Islands (Dendroglyphs)*, 1887
Sepia monochrome, 225 × 290mm
Signed and dated lower left: M.O.S. 1887
Exhibition: CSA Winter Exhibition of Black and White Pictures 1887, 92 Moriori Tree
Carving, Chatham Islands £2
Canterbury Museum, Christchurch

*13. Mountain Lily (*Ranunculus lyalli*), (c. 1885)
Watercolour over traces of pencil 480 × 360mm
Collection of the Troup Family

14. (Image unavailable at time of publication.)
Study of New Zealand Coltsfoot and View of Canterbury Plains, 1885
Watercolour, 490 × 370mm
Signed and dated upper right: M.O. Stoddart 1885
Collection of Jenny and Ian Bishop

*15. Mandevilla, 1888
Watercolour and bodycolour, 470 × 310mm
Signed and dated lower left: M.O.S. 1888
Exhibition: CSA Annual 1888, 220 Mandevilla £4 10s
Collection of Justin Hobbs, Esq.

*16. Cherry Blossom, 1890
Watercolour over pencil, 440 × 345mm
Signed and dated lower left: M.O.S. 1890
Exhibition: CSA Annual 1890, 126 Cherry Blossom £4 4s
Private Collection

*17. Primroses, also known as *Primroses and Apple Blossom,* 1891

Watercolour over pencil, 514 × 335mm
Signed and dated lower left: M.O.S. 1891
Exhibition: CSA Annual 1892, 110 Primroses £6 6s; ASA. Annual 1892, 117 Primroses £6
Collection of School of Fine Arts, University of Canterbury, Christchurch

18. Christmas Roses, 1893

Watercolour, 514 × 677mm
Signed and dated lower right: M.O.S. 1893
Exhibition: NZAFA Annual 1893, 51 Christmas Roses £6
Presented by Mr Gladstone Hutton, 1961
Collection of Hocken Library, University of Otago, Dunedin

*19. Apple Blossom, (c. 1897)

Watercolour and bodycolour, 655 × 497mm
Signed and dated lower left: M.O. Stoddart 1897
Collection of Christchurch Polytechnic, Te Whare Runanga o Otautahi

20. First Flowers of Spring, also known as *Spring Flowers,* (c. 1902-06)

Watercolour and bodycolour, 382 × 555mm
Signed lower left: M.O. Stoddart
Exhibition: CSA Annual 1907, 283 First Flowers of Spring £7 7s
Bequeathed by Helen Dorothy Feaver, 1965
Collection of Robert McDougall Art Gallery, Christchurch

*21. Christmas Roses, 1906

Watercolour and bodycolour, 445 × 590mm
Signed and dated lower right: M.O. Stoddart 1906
Exhibition: Paris, Société Nationale des Beaux-Arts, 1906, 1678 Les roses de Noël
Private Collection

*22. Spring Flowers, Cornwall, also known as *Narcissi and White Daffodils,*
     (c. 1902-06)

Watercolour and bodycolour, 590 × 465mm
Signed lower left: M.O. Stoddart
Exhibition: ASA Annual 1907, 174 Spring Flowers, Cornwall £10 10s
Bequeathed by Helen Dorothy Feaver, 1965
Collection of Robert McDougall Art Gallery, Christchurch

*23. Anna Ollivier Roses, (c.1912)

Watercolour and bodycolour, 395 × 540mm
Signed lower left: (brushpoint black) M.O. Stoddart and below (brushpoint red)
M.O. Stoddart
Exhibition: CSA Annual 1912, 289 Anna Ollivier Roses £9 9s
Presented by the Canterbury Society of Arts 1932
Collection of Robert McDougall Art Gallery, Christchurch

*24. Bowl of Roses

Watercolour and bodycolour, 460 × 590mm
Signed lower left: M.O. Stoddart
Bequeathed by Miss Maude Isabella Mary Haines, 1971
Collection of Dunedin Public Art Gallery

+25. Roses, also known as *Roses (White),* (c.1924)

Watercolour and charcoal, 393 × 570mm
Signed lower right: M.O. Stoddart
Exhibited: NZAFA, Annual 1924, 205 Roses £10 10s
Collection of the Museum of New Zealand Te Papa Tongarewa
Gift of the New Zealand Academy of Fine Arts, 1936
Negative no. B041185

*26. Camellias

Watercolour and bodycolour, 460 × 615mm
Signed lower left: M.O. Stoddart
Presented by Mrs Kathleen Kirkby, 1992
Collection of Anderson Park Art Gallery Society Inc., Invercargill

*27. Violets

Watercolour and bodycolour, 380 × 560mm
Signed lower left: M.O. Stoddart
W.S. & Alison MacGibbon Collection, University of Canterbury, Christchurch

28. Canterbury Plains from Dyers Pass Road, 1888

Watercolour and pencil, 270 × 375mm
Signed and dated lower right: M.O.S. 1888
Purchased with assistance from the Olive Stirrat Bequest, 1987
Collection of Robert McDougall Art Gallery, Christchurch

29. Sumner Beach, 1893

Watercolour, 360 × 520mm
Signed and dated lower left: M.O. Stoddart 1893
Private Collection

30. On the Beach, Cheviot, 1896

Watercolour and bodycolour, 392 × 565mm
Signed and dated lower right: M.O. Stoddart 1896
Exhibition: OAS Annual 1896, 176 On the Beach, Cheviot £4 4s
Collection of Dunedin Public Art Gallery

*31. Harbour, St Ives, (c. 1902-06)

Watercolour and bodycolour over charcoal, 470 × 595mm
Signed lower left: M.O. Stoddart
Exhibition: CSA Annual 1907, 205 Harbour, St Ives £15 15s
Private Collection

32. The Moors, (c. 1902-06)

Watercolour and bodycolour, 258 × 355mm
Signed lower left: M.O. Stoddart
Collection of Robert McDougall Art Gallery, Christchurch

33. Blossom, 1902

Watercolour and bodycolour, 460 × 585mm
Signed lower left: M.O. Stoddart 1902
Private Collection

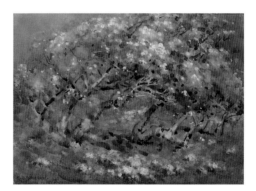

34. Old Cornish Orchard, also known as *Plum Blossom,* (c.1902)

Watercolour and bodycolour, 255 × 355mm
Signed lower left: M.O. Stoddart
Collection of the Christchurch Polytechnic, Te Whare Runanga o Otautahi

*35. Apple Blossom, (c. 1902-06)
Watercolour and bodycolour over charcoal, 435 × 540mm
Signed lower right: M.O. Stoddart
Southland Museum and Art Gallery, Niho o te Taniwha
Collection of Southland Art Gallery Trust Board

*36. Spring Blossom, (c. 1906)
Watercolour and bodycolour, 455 × 610mm
Signed lower left: M.O. Stoddart
Presented in memory of Lady Allen, 1943
Collection of the Dunedin Public Art Gallery

*37. Bluebells, (c.1902-1906)
Watercolour and bodycolour, 240 × 340mm
Signed lower left: M.O. Stoddart
Private Collection

*38. Storm Clouds, Blythburgh, Suffolk, also known as *Suffolk Village,* (c.1905-06)
Watercolour and bodycolour, 255 × 360mm
Signed lower left: M.O. Stoddart
Exhibition: Christchurch, New Zealand International Exhibition, 1906-07, 276 Storm
Clouds, Blythburgh, Suffolk £ 5 5s
Collection of Robert McDougall Art Gallery, Christchurch

39. A Suffolk Lane, also known as *A Surrey Lane,* (c. 1905-06)
Watercolour and bodycolour over charcoal, 240 × 345mm
Signed lower left: M.O. Stoddart
Exhibition: OAS Annual 1907, 238 A Suffolk Road £5 5s; Nelson, Suter Art Society
Exhibition, 1919
Presented by Mrs R.S. Duncan
Collection of Bishop Suter Art Gallery, Nelson

40. Stable at Diamond Harbour, (c.1907-13)
Watercolour and bodycolour over charcoal, 255 × 355mm
Signed lower left: M.O. Stoddart
Bradshaw Collection, Canterbury Museum, Christchurch

*41. *Landscape with Wood and Sheep,* (c.1907-13)

Watercolour and bodycolour, 280 × 388mm
Signed lower left: M.O. Stoddart
Presented by Mrs S.M. Winn, 1964
Auckland Art Gallery Collection

*42. *Diamond Harbour,* 1909

Watercolour and bodycolour over charcoal, 255 × 355mm
Signed and dated lower left: M.O. Stoddart 1909
Collection of Christchurch Civic Art Gallery Trust

*43. *The Old Almond Tree, Diamond Harbour*

Watercolour and bodycolour over charcoal, 235 × 340mm
Signed lower left: M.O. Stoddart
W.S. & Alison MacGibbon Collection, University of Canterbury, Christchurch

*44. *Old Homestead, Diamond Harbour,* (c. 1913)

Watercolour and bodycolour over charcoal, 383 × 494mm
Signed lower left: M.O. Stoddart
Exhibition: CSA Annual 1913, 293 Old Homestead, Diamond Harbour £9 9s
Collection of Robert McDougall Art Gallery, Christchurch

45. *Old Homestead, Diamond Harbour,* (c.1913)

Watercolour and bodycolour over charcoal, 250 × 350mm
Signed lower left: M.O. Stoddart
Private Collection

46. *Old Homestead, Diamond Harbour,* (c.1913)

Watercolour and bodycolour over charcoal, 230 × 310mm
Signed lower left: M.O. Stoddart
Private Collection

*47. Godley House, Diamond Harbour, (c. 1913)
Watercolour and bodycolour over charcoal, 382 x 505mm
Signed lower left: M.O. Stoddart
Purchased with assistance from the Olive Stirrat Bequest, 1990
Collection of Robert McDougall Art Gallery, Christchurch

48. A Corner of my Garden, (c.1911)
Watercolour and bodycolour over charcoal, 320 x 460mm
Signed lower right: M.O. Stoddart
Exhibition: NZAFA Annual 1911, 162 A Corner of my Garden £5 5s
Private Collection

49. Garden, Christchurch, (c.1912)
Watercolour and bodycolour over charcoal, 254 x 354mm
Signed lower left: M.O. Stoddart
Exhibition: CSA Annual 1912, 207 Garden, Christchurch £5 5s
Collection of Hocken Library, University of Otago, Dunedin

50. A Garden, Cashmere Hills, (c.1915)
Watercolour and bodycolour over charcoal, 370 x 490mm
Signed lower left: M.O. Stoddart
Exhibition: CSA Annual, 1915, 162 A Garden, Cashmere Hills £9 9s
Collection of Susan Mary Johnstone, *née* Baker

*51. House in a Summer Garden
Watercolour and bodycolour over charcoal, 242 x 342mm
Signed lower left: M.O. Stoddart
Collection of Forrester Gallery, Oamaru, gifted by the North Otago Art Society

52. The Drive in Summer
Watercolour and bodycolour over charcoal, 245 x 355mm
Signed lower left: M.O. Stoddart
Private Collection

53. Blossom, Worcester St Bridge

Watercolour and bodycolour over charcoal, 255 × 346mm
Signed lower left: M.O. Stoddart
Collection of Robert McDougall Art Gallery, Christchurch

+54. Riverside, Autumn, also known as *Autumn River Scene,* and *Autumn,* (c. 1930)

Watercolour and charcoal on paper on tan cardboard, 461 × 583mm
Signed lower left: M.O. Stoddart
Gift of D.A. Ewan, 1942
Collection of the Museum of New Zealand Te Papa Tongarewa
Negative no. B037388

55. The Almond Tree, Clifton, Sumner, (c. 1916)

Watercolour and bodycolour over charcoal, 255 × 357mm
Signed lower left: M.O. Stoddart
Exhibition: OAS Annual 1916, 267 The Almond Tree, Clifton, Sumner £5 5; CSA Annual
1917, 270 The Almond Tree, Clifton, Sumner £5 5s
Collection of Waikato Museum of Art and History, Te Whare Taonga o Waikato, Hamilton

*56. The Estuary

Watercolour, 245 × 345mm
Signed lower left: M.O. Stoddart
Private Collection

*57. Sandhills

Watercolour and bodycolour over charcoal, 265 × 375mm
Signed lower left: M.O. Stoddart
Collection of Anderson Park Art Gallery Society Inc., Invercargill

58. Sand Dunes, (c. 1920)

Watercolour and bodycolour over charcoal, 245 × 345mm
Signed lower left: M.O. Stoddart
Collection of Rangi Ruru Girls' School, Christchurch

*59. Yellow Lupins, (c.1925)
Watercolour and bodycolour over charcoal, 450 x 480mm
Signed lower left: M.O. Stoddart
Collection of Manawatu Art Gallery, Palmerston North

*60. Bush Fire, Paraparaumu, (c.1908)
Watercolour and bodycolour, 255 x 355mm
Signed lower left: M.O. Stoddart
Collection of Robert McDougall Art Gallery, Christchurch

*61. Sheep Country, (c.1916)
Watercolour and bodycolour over charcoal, 240 x 355mm
Signed lower left: M.O. Stoddart
Exhibition: Suter Art Society, 1919
Presented by Mrs R.S. Duncan
Collection of Bishop Suter Art Gallery, Nelson

*62. Gisborne from Te Karaka
Watercolour and bodycolour over charcoal, 255 x 356mm
Signed lower left: M.O. Stoddart
Collection of Waikato Museum of Art and History, Te Whare Taonga o Waikato,
Hamilton

63. Bridge over the Kowhai, (c.1920-c.1930)
Watercolour and bodycolour over charcoal, 450 x 485mm
Signed lower left: M.O. Stoddart
Presented by the artist, 1933
Collection of the Christchurch Polytechnic, Te Whare Runanga o Otautahi

+64. Old Cottage, (Otira), also known as *Old Cottage, Arthur's Pass,* (c.1927)
Watercolour and bodycolour over charcoal, 482 x 630mm
Signed lower left: M.O. Stoddart
Exhibition: Christchurch, Exhibition of Paintings by the Late Miss Stoddart, 1935, 56 Old
Cottage (Otira) £15 15s
Gifted to the National Art Gallery by the NZAFA; 1936
Collection of the Museum of New Zealand Te Papa Tongarewa
Negative no. B037389

*65. *Cabbage Trees, Clarence Valley, Kaikoura*
Watercolour and bodycolour over charcoal, 455 × 530mm
Signed lower left: M.O. Stoddart
Presented by Lady Isaac, 1996
Collection of Christchurch Civic Art Gallery Trust

*66. *In the Mackenzie Country,* (c.1930)
Watercolour and bodycolour over charcoal, 480 × 625mm
Signed lower left: M.O. Stoddart
Presented by the Canterbury Society of Arts, 1932
Collection of Robert McDougall Art Gallery, Christchurch

67. *Looking up the Otira Valley towards Mount Rolleston*
Watercolour and bodycolour over charcoal, 430 × 470mm
Signed lower left: M.O. Stoddart
Private Collection

*68. *Mountain Lilies*
Watercolour and bodycolour over charcoal, 458 × 480mm
Signed lower left: M.O. Stoddart
Collection of Christchurch Civic Art Gallery Trust

*69. *An Otira Stream,* also known as *Mountain Rata,* (c. 1927)
Watercolour and bodycolour over charcoal, 430 × 460mm
Signed lower left: M.O. Stoddart
Collection of Robert McDougall Art Gallery, Christchurch

+70. *Stocking Glacier from Hooker Valley,* also known as *Snow-Stocking
Glacier,* and as *Mountain Heights, New Zealand,* (c.1932)
Watercolour and bodycolour over charcoal, 478 × 438mm
Signed lower right: M.O. Stoddart
Exhibited: CSA Annual 1932, 100 Stocking Glacier from Hooker Valley
£15 15s
Presented to the National Art Gallery, 1936
Collection of the Museum of New Zealand Te Papa Tongarewa
Negative no. B037393

+71. *View of Mount Cook*

Watercolour and bodycolour over charcoal, 508 × 457mm
Signed lower left: M.O. Stoddart
Collection of the Museum of New Zealand Te Papa Tongarewa
Negative no. B041177

*72. *Mount Sefton*

Watercolour and bodycolour over charcoal, 445 × 585mm
Signed lower left: M.O. Stoddart
Collection of Robert McDougall Art Gallery, Christchurch

*73. *View of Mount Cook*

Watercolour and bodycolour over charcoal, 450 × 480mm
Signed lower left: M.O. Stoddart
Auckland Art Gallery Collection
Purchased 1935